SIXTY
DAYS IN COMBAT

D0802491

SIXTY
DAYS IN COMBAT

AN INFANTRYMAN'S MEMOIR OF WORLD WAR II IN EUROPE

DEAN P. JOY

PRESIDIO
PRESS

BALLANTINE BOOKS • NEW YORK

A Presidio Press Book
Published by The Random House Publishing Group
Copyright © 2004 by Dean P. Joy

All rights reserved under International and Pan-American
Copyright Conventions. Published in the United States by
The Random House Publishing Group, a division of
Random House, Inc., New York, and simultaneously in
Canada by Random House of Canada Limited, Toronto.

No part of this book may be reproduced or transmitted in any
form or by any means, electronic or mechanical, including
photocopying, recording, or by any information storage and
retrieval system, without permission in writing from the publisher.

Presidio Press and colophon are trademarks
of Random House, Inc.

www.presidiopress.com

Library of Congress Cataloging-in-Publication Data is
available upon request from the publisher.

ISBN 0-89141-839-3

Book design by Julie Schroeder

Manufactured in the United States of America

First Edition: March 2004

1 3 5 7 9 10 8 6 4 2

This memoir is for Annie

———

And it is also written in memory of my mother and father, who saved each and every one of the hundreds of letters I wrote home during the three and one-half years I served in the Army of the United States, from June 1943 through November 1946. Those letters, together with a small diary I kept, and my copy of *The History of the U.S. Army 71st Infantry Division*, have been invaluable in sharpening my recollection of places, characters, events, and dates recorded herein.

CENTRAL ARKANSAS LIBRARY SYSTEM
LITTLE ROCK PUBLIC LIBRARY
100 ROCK STREET
LITTLE ROCK, ARKANSAS 72201

Contents

AUTHOR'S NOTE
▪ xi ▪

PROLOGUE
▪ xiii ▪

PART ONE: RELUCTANT VOLUNTEER
June 12, 1942, to March 6, 1945
▪ 1 ▪

CHAPTER 1: FROM COLLEGE FRESHMAN TO ARMY DRAFTEE
June 12, 1942, through July 2, 1943
▪ 3 ▪

CHAPTER 2: THE U.S. ARMY AIR CORPS
July through September 1943
▪ 10 ▪

CHAPTER 3: THE ASTP AT MOSCOW
October 1943 to March 1944
▪ 21 ▪

CHAPTER 4: HUNTER-LIGGETT MILITARY RESERVATION
April and May 1944
▪ 27 ▪

CHAPTER 5: FORT BENNING
May 25, 1944, to January 11, 1945
▪ 38 ▪

CHAPTER 6: CAMP KILMER AND THE USS *GENERAL TASKER BLISS*
January 12 to February 6, 1945
• 47 •

CHAPTER 7: LE HAVRE, CAMP OLD GOLD, AND THE ANCIENT SMELL OF
FRANCE
February 6 to March 6, 1945
• 55 •

PART TWO: COMBAT INFANTRYMAN
March 6 to May 8, 1945
• 67 •

CHAPTER 8: TO THE FRONT BY RAIL, TRUCK, AND JEEP
March 6 to 11, 1945
• 69 •

CHAPTER 9: THE FRONT AT SKYLINE DRIVE
Sunday, March 11, 1945
• 78 •

CHAPTER 10: FIRST TIME UNDER FIRE
Sunday, March 11, 1945
• 86 •

CHAPTER 11: FIRST FIRE MISSIONS
Monday, March 12, 1945
• 95 •

CHAPTER 12: FIRST CASUALTIES AND CLOSE CONTACTS WITH THE
ENEMY
Tuesday, Wednesday, and Thursday, March 13, 14, and 15, 1945
• 104 •

CHAPTER 13: THROUGH THE MINEFIELD TO THE SIEGFRIED LINE
Friday, March 16, through Thursday, March 22, 1945
• 116 •

CHAPTER 14: CARNAGE AT PIRMASENS
Friday and Saturday, March 23 and 24, 1945
• 129 •

Contents

CHAPTER 15: THE BATTLE FOR GERMERSHEIM AND LINGENFELD
Sunday, March 25, 1945
* 135 *

CHAPTER 16: POSTMORTEM ON THE RHINE, AND TRANSFER TO
PATTON'S THIRD ARMY
Monday, March 26, through Saturday, March 31, 1945
* 153 *

CHAPTER 17: BUDINGER WALD AND THE 6TH SS MOUNTAIN DIVISION
NORD
Sunday, April 1, through Wednesday, April 4, 1945
* 168 *

CHAPTER 18: A LETTER HOME, THE WAREHOUSE AT FULDA, AND ON TO
COBURG
Thursday, April 5, through Wednesday, April 11, 1945
* 184 *

CHAPTER 19: COBURG, BAYREUTH, PEGNITZ, AND A ROADBLOCK IN THE
FOREST
Thursday, April 12, through Friday, April 20, 1945
* 194 *

CHAPTER 20: THE DANUBE WASN'T BLUE
Saturday, April 21, through Monday, April 30, 1945
* 214 *

CHAPTER 21: THE LAST BATTLES
Tuesday, May 1, through Tuesday, May 8, 1945
* 237 *

EPILOGUE
* 260 *

More than a half-century has passed since the events recorded here took place. Time has not erased my memory of key events, scenes, or the faces of the men involved. In part this is because I was among the lucky survivors who suffered no physical wounds and saw just enough infantry combat to be able to tell my war stories to those who are interested. And in part, my memory is sharp because those sixty days were by far the most profound of my life—they left deeper and more indelible scars on my psyche than any of the events that have happened to me since.

I would surely have forgotten many names of people and towns, and could never have remembered the exact dates and days of the week, if I had not kept the little notebook diary, and if my parents had not saved all the letters I wrote. And, of course, the 71st Division history book, with its description of battles and its many photographs, was invaluable.

Also, I am fortunate to have some ability as an amateur sketch artist, and to be married to an accomplished professional artist. She believes, as I do, that a picture is worth a thousand words, and strongly suggested that I should illustrate these memoirs with sketches of selected scenes that stick in my memory, as if my eye had been a camera.

Even so, from this distance in time, I sometimes found it difficult to paint a clear portrait of myself in combat. It has not been easy to capture how immature, frightened, lonely, and disappointed a young man I was in those bygone days. And it is ironic to recall how hard I tried to avoid the infantry, and how desperately I hoped to be a pilot and fly P-51 Mustang fighters in the U.S. Army Air Forces.

I was born in July 1924, in Denver, Colorado—the eldest son in a family of four children. My parents, both Presbyterians from Iowa farms, had come to Denver in 1920. My older sister and two younger brothers and I were raised lovingly, seldom punished, and never once heard our parents argue, even when times were hard during the Depression years.

We loved our mother dearly. Dorothy Porter Joy was a sweet little woman with a nice singing voice. Each of us was lucky to have inherited her musical ear. Her Scotch-Irish father and Welsh mother had both died before she came of age. As the sixth of eight children, she knew what it was to work hard to make ends meet. Let it be said that none of her four children ever went hungry or wore rags when money was short. Like two or three of her sisters, she had a two-year college education at Iowa State Teachers' College, and taught in a one-room Iowa country schoolhouse before she married Dad in 1918.

But if we loved our mother, it must be said that we absolutely *adored* our Scotch-Irish father! Warren Witherall Joy was a farm boy with three older brothers and a younger sister. He and Mother were high school sweethearts. Inasmuch as the Iowa farm on which he was born was not large enough to split among several children, he decided to pursue a career in mechanical engineering, and worked his way through four years at Iowa State

College in Ames. He married Mother in April 1918, then went off to World War I, serving as a junior engineer on Merchant Marine freighters and tankers. He made several trips to France in convoys, and after the war, in 1920, he and Mother moved to Denver, where he founded a small sales engineering company specializing in steam power-plant equipment, ranging from small valves and instruments to huge steam boilers. His company existed on commissions earned whenever competitive bids by teams of larger manufacturing companies he helped organize won contracts for power plants and coal mining equipment in Colorado, New Mexico, Wyoming, Utah, and other western states.

Although never wealthy, Dad was generous to a fault, especially with three of Mother's less fortunate sisters and three of her fatherless nephews. He had a great sense of humor but seldom made small talk, and I was always in awe of his quiet wisdom. In my eyes he could do nothing wrong—he was my god.

When my parents moved to Denver they bought a small wood-frame bungalow on a corner lot in the University Park area, near the University of Denver. Just before the crash of 1929—when my sister, Kathleen, was seven, I was five, and my brother Stanley was a year old—we moved to a somewhat larger three-bedroom brick house on a corner lot not far from Washington Park Elementary School. We lived there during the worst of the Depression. My youngest brother, Donald, was born in 1934, when I was ten years old.

By 1936 Dad's income was sufficient to buy a larger two-story house on a corner lot just across the street from Washington Park, and only a few blocks from South High School. That was my home until June 1943, when, eighteen months after Pearl Harbor brought us into the war, I finished my freshman year in the engineering college at the University of Colorado, and volunteered for induction into the Army of the United States. I was three weeks shy of my nineteenth birthday when I left for the service.

This memoir is divided into two parts: Part One covers my Stateside army service and the deployment of my infantry division to France; Part Two is a day-by-day chronicle of my two months in combat, from March 10 through May 8, 1945.

SIXTY
DAYS IN COMBAT

PART I

RELUCTANT VOLUNTEER

JUNE 12, 1942, TO MARCH 6, 1945

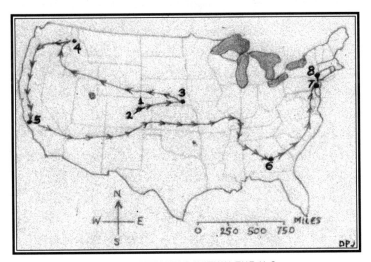

MY ARMY TRAVELS WITHIN THE U.S.
FROM 2 JULY 1943 THROUGH 6 MARCH 1943

1. Denver —————————————————7.2.43
2. Fort Logan ————————————7.2 to 7.9.43
3. Lincoln AFB ————————————— 7.10 to 10.2.43
4. ASTP U of Idaho ——————— 10.4.43 to 3.29.44
5. Hunter-Liggett Mil Res, CA ——— 4.2 to 5.20.44
6. Fort Benning, GA ——————5.25.44 to 1.12.45
7. Camp Kilmer, NJ ———————— 1.13 to 1.25.45
8. Staten Island, NY————————————1.26.45

CHAPTER 1

FROM COLLEGE FRESHMAN TO ARMY DRAFTEE

June 12, 1942, through July 2, 1943

Like my boyhood friend Horace Jeffrey—we called him Jeff—I had a passion for airplanes. But unlike him, I had never made plans to go to college. To my father's dismay, I had not taken one of the high school math courses needed to enter college as an engineering student. I felt my talents were limited to drawing, commercial art, and playing the clarinet. In high school my plans for a career were to become either a commercial artist, or maybe a cartoonist, or maybe a jazz clarinetist, or possibly even an airline pilot.

It was on a June day that summer of 1942, just after I graduated from high school, that Dad invited me to join him downtown for lunch. He asked me if I would consider getting a college engineering degree—perhaps at his alma mater, Iowa State College—and someday take over his small business. I painfully declined, suggesting that either of my two younger brothers would be a better choice when the time came. "Dad," I said, "you have many years before you may want to retire. And to be honest, if I went to college I would only be interested in aeronautical engineering, not mechanical. I'm not cut out to follow in your footsteps as a power plant sales engineer."

He understood, and from that point on it was tacitly understood that my brother Stanley would one day take over the business. But I was faced with a dilemma. On July 21, my eighteenth birthday, I would be eligible for the draft, and unless in college I was almost certain to be called up before the end of the year and sent to the dreaded infantry—in my mind the dirtiest, least glamorous military service imaginable. I gave no thought to joining the navy; I was a poor swimmer. Like thousands of other draft-age American boys, I dreamed of flying P-51 Mustang fighter aircraft with the U.S. Army Air Corps.

At Jeff's suggestion, I went with him on a trip to the registrar's office at the University of Colorado in Boulder, and was told that I would be accepted as an engineering freshman that fall if I passed a summer night class in solid geometry. I had found a summer job running an ancient knitting machine at Gates Rubber Company, making radiator hose for tank engines. My pay was all of forty-four cents per hour, and I spent most of it taking flying lessons and attending a night school class in solid geometry. By summer's end I had accumulated just five hours in a little Piper Cub when my flight instructor was called off to join the Civil Air Patrol. I was almost broke, and that ended my first shot at getting a pilot's license. It wasn't until 1948, courtesy of the GI Bill, that I earned that coveted license.

Dad and Mother had been carefully saving enough money to send all four of us children to college. My piano-playing sister was well on her way to a degree in music at Colorado College. And now, in August 1942, Dad agreed to pay for my college education in aeronautical engineering at the University of Colorado. And so it was that in mid-September Jeff and I became roommates in an old widow's rooming house within walking distance of the CU campus in Boulder. The main attraction of the newly formed School of Aeronautical Engineering was an expert who had been hired away from Purdue University to head it. His name was Professor Karl D. Wood, better known to us all as K. D.— author of *Technical Aerodynamics,* probably the best textbook in the field at that time.

On the war fronts, while Jeff and I struggled through our first months as freshman engineering students, Russia was holding off the German armies in front of Moscow, the British had stopped Rommel at El Alamein in Egypt, and the hated Japanese in the Pacific were licking their wounds after their disastrous defeat at Midway. Our navy was building up its strength with new, fast carriers, battleships, cruisers, and destroyers now coming off the ways at record rates. And General Douglas MacArthur was getting ready to take the offensive from bases in Australia.

The name Dwight Eisenhower was not yet on the front pages, although he had just been given two stars and would become famous as commander of the forthcoming invasion of North Africa. Nor was George Patton yet famous, although—like MacArthur— he was a prima donna with an insatiable love of personal publicity. But in my opinion the similarities between these two egotists ended there. Patton was perhaps a bit crazy, but he was a tactical genius who loved to fight and whose troops both feared and respected him. On the other hand, MacArthur was a much-ridiculed tin god and obnoxious snob who thought of himself as the world's best global strategist. I believed then, and still believe today, that he fancied himself a president—perhaps even king.

At Christmastime in 1942 I came home for a welcome respite from the spartan life and colder climate of Boulder, where I could never seem to stay warm. My mother invited a couple of GIs for Christmas dinner, responding to a call from Central Presbyterian Church, and it was of considerable interest to me to hear them talk about army life. I could not know it, of course, but that winter holiday of 1942 was to be the last I would spend at home until four years later, when I returned from the war as a twenty-two-year-old veteran wearing the coveted Combat Infantryman's Badge and platoon sergeant's stripes.

During the Easter break in the spring of 1943 I rode the train to Denver and joined our family at the Easter sunrise services up in the huge amphitheater of Red Rocks Park. From every seat of that amphitheater one could watch the sun rise over Denver as the city lights blinked out. I remember wondering, as I looked over the Plains toward Nebraska, if my fate would take me across the Atlantic to Europe, or west to the Pacific, when my number was called.

Before returning to Boulder, I rode with Dad on a business trip to Colorado Springs. We talked about the war and my hope to join the Army Air Corps. En route we passed close to Camp Carson and spotted several hundred khaki-clad infantrymen hiking toward Pike's Peak, leading long strings of heavily laden mules. I could not know that this was the same outfit with which I would serve in combat only ten months later. Those slogging GIs belonged to the 5th Infantry Regiment, part of the newly organized 71st Light Infantry Division.

In June 1943 I completed my freshman year in engineering at CU with a B average. The big question was whether I would be drafted before completing a second year. Desperate to know where I stood, I borrowed my mother's car, drove down to the Denver draft board, and put the question to an old gentleman. He looked at a file and informed me that, as I would turn nineteen in July, my number would almost surely be called by November, even if I had started my sophomore year.

Disappointed, I asked, "How do I go about volunteering for the Army Air Corps? I would like to fly, but I would be happy as a crewman, or even as an aircraft engine mechanic. *Anything* rather than being sent to the infantry."

"That's easy," the old gentleman said. "Volunteer for early induction today and you can choose your branch. But if you wait until November there's no such guarantee. I can set your physical up for this week, and if you pass you'll be called in July."

I said I'd take a walk and think it over. I walked around the block, agonizing whether to go to my father's office for his advice. Then I thought: No, this decision is mine alone. Half an hour later I had made up my mind. I returned to the draft board and signed the papers. It was a month before my nineteenth birthday. That night my parents tried to hide their pain when I told them I had volunteered to be drafted five months early to avoid being sent straight to the dreaded infantry.

Two days later I drove downtown to take the physical, which I nearly flunked. First, a little hammertoe on my left foot attracted a team of three doctors, who had me walk naked, back and forth, with and without shoes. My heart fell as they deliberated. "Oh, no sir," I assured the senior doctor. "It doesn't bother me! I walk without a limp. See? I was a Boy Scout, I play tennis, I'm a fast runner, and I climb mountains with the Colorado Mountain Climbing Club." It was all true. So they smiled and passed me.

The second problem was an unsuspected polyp in one of my nostrils, discovered by an ear, nose, and throat specialist in the line of examiners. "That's bad," he said. My heart fell again as the specialist wrote something on the form. But the last doctor in the line looked over the form, signed it, and said, "Passed with flying colors. Get dressed, take this form to the next room, and wait for the next swearing-in."

What a relief! Army Air Corps, here I come, I said to myself. The thought of being classified 4-F (physically unfit for military service) and seeing the unspoken question "Young man, why aren't you in the service like my son?" on countless faces I would pass on the street was almost as horrible as the thought of serving in the infantry.

Little did I know that before the war ended my questionable feet would carry me many hundreds of miles across Europe as a lowly infantryman.

My orders were to report at the induction center on July 2, 1943. That morning I brought my single suitcase down the stairs, hugged my brothers and kissed my sister good-bye with studied nonchalance, then went out on the front porch with my mother as Dad pulled the car around to the front of the house. Wonder of wonders, Mother smiled bravely and shed not one tear that I could see. Our embrace was quick, I strode thankfully to the car, turned just once to wave, and then off we drove. I have no doubt that she cried after we were gone.

Ten minutes later we pulled up in front of the induction center in downtown Denver. What happened there at the curb was totally unexpected. Still playing the cool grown-up, I shook my

A TEARFUL GOOD-BYE TO MY FATHER

father's hand and said something like, "See you, Dad. Don't worry. I'll write home often." My beloved Rock of Gibraltar father opened his mouth but could not speak as tears rolled down his cheek! I knew he was trying to say, "I love you, son," but nothing came except a sob of grief. Unwanted tears welled in my own eyes, and now it was I who couldn't speak.

I put my hand on his shoulder, turned wordlessly, got out of the car, and with suitcase in hand rushed into the building through a crowd of onlooking draftees. That was the only time I ever saw my father cry until just before he died, in June 1976, thirty-three years later.

CHAPTER 2

THE U.S. ARMY AIR CORPS

July through September 1943

There must have been more than a hundred of us seated on folding chairs in a large room in the Denver induction center. A sergeant came in and bawled, "Awright, all you guys who wanna be pilots, stand up!" About half of us gullible new draftees stood up, and the others had a good laugh when the sergeant said, "Okay, each of you pilots fold up yer chair and pile it up on that stack over there, then come back and git the other chairs."

When we were done with that chore, we were all lined up alphabetically and given name tags for our suitcases. Shortly after that, several army buses drove up in front of the center and we climbed aboard. I spotted a few familiar faces from South High School in the crowd but recognized no one from the University of Colorado. The hackneyed phrase "You're in the army now" kept going through my mind as the convoy of buses pulled out and headed for the processing center at Fort Logan, near the suburb of Englewood, southwest of Denver.

The day had started bright and sunny, but by the time the convoy entered the Fort Logan gate, huge cumulus clouds were piling up, and the mountains to the west were obscured. We unloaded in a large parking lot and formed a ragged line under the direction of a sergeant and two corporals in sun helmets and suntan uniforms. After a long wait, an officer arrived in a jeep and the sergeant reported, "Company B present and accounted for, sir." The officer made a short speech of welcome, then left as the wind rose and the first raindrops began to fall. We recruits were soaked by the time the noncoms double-timed us down to the new white barracks, where we left our suitcases. Then we were run back up a hill to the mess hall for our first army meal.

After lunch we were issued summer Class A suntan uniforms with cap, tie, a web belt with brass buckle, green army fatigues and fatigue hat, two pairs of GI shoes, olive-drab socks, shorts, and undershirts, two barracks bags, one mattress cover, two towels, and a bar of yellow GI soap. Back at our barracks the sergeant passed out copies of *The Soldier's Handbook* and told us we had twenty-four hours to memorize the General Orders by heart and learn how to salute. A corporal showed us how to arrange our gear in the green footlockers, told us what civilian personal items we could keep, and gave us ten minutes to get out of our civvies into our olive-green fatigues, and repack our suitcases with stuff to be sent home. He reappeared with a pfc carrying pails, brooms, mops, and rags, and we new recruits were put to work mopping the floors and dusting shelves, windowsills, and double-tiered bunks.

Three of my friends from South High were in my barracks, all with orders assuring us that we would be sent to the Army Air Corps. These were Stan Detrick, Bill Bromm, and Gordon Bungaard. We four picked bunks close to one another and helped each other make up our bunks in army fashion, as demonstrated by a corporal—blankets tucked with "hospital" folds at the foot and stretched tight so that a dropped coin would bounce. Bungaard, who had been in high school ROTC, showed us how to salute properly, with elbow forward and forearm and hand swept up to the forehead in a straight line. By the time we marched to evening chow I had accepted the fact that I was no longer a civilian but a soldier in Uncle Sam's army.

My first few days as an army recruit at Fort Logan were doubtless not much different than for several million other American draftees in World War II. There were forms to fill out, paybooks and dog tags to be issued, typhoid and tetanus shots, GI haircuts, and a variety of written tests. An assembly was held for the reading of the Articles of War, including the dire warning that the penalty for wartime desertion in the face of the enemy is death.

Hours not otherwise occupied with close-order drill or picking up trash—known as policing the grounds—were spent studying *The Soldier's Handbook* to memorize the General Orders. These were like the Ten Commandments, and had to be recited on demand of any noncom or officer of the guard, especially when approached while on night duty as a fire guard armed with a billy club.

Today, all I can remember of these orders is a parody on the one dealing with fire and danger. It goes: "In case of fire, ring the bell. In case of danger, run like hell!"

Seven days after arriving at Fort Logan, about a hundred of us who were slated for the Army Air Corps were alerted to be shipped out. We were not told our destination—only that we would board a train at Denver Union Station that night, a Wednesday.

Rumor had it that we were going to Texas or someplace else in the Deep South, possibly Florida. At the station we were given box lunches before boarding the train, and I managed to buy a map of all U.S. rail lines. In my wallet I carried a map of army bases that I had clipped from a newspaper. With these treasures I planned to plot our route and guess our destination before arrival.

While we waited to file out to the train, we had our first look at the enemy. A group of sullen German prisoners of war with

FIREGUARD RECRUIT RECITING A GENERAL ORDER

POW stenciled on the backs of their desert uniforms were marched through the station, guarded by MPs with tommy guns. You can imagine the impression that made on us new recruits. One of our sergeants spoke to the MP in charge, then came back and told us that the Krauts were from Rommel's Afrika Korps and had been captured in Tunisia two months earlier. Now they were on their way to pick sugar beets someplace in eastern Colorado for the duration of the war.

We could hardly believe our good luck when we saw that the entire train was made up of Pullman sleeper cars. Several of my companions agreed with my logic that the trip would surely take more than one night, or we would be riding in day coaches. I figured that if the train trip lasted at least two nights and a day, at an average speed of fifty miles per hour, allowing for a fifteen-minute stop every hundred miles or so, our destination had to be at least fifteen hundred miles distant. This ruled out Texas or California. We must be headed east, I reasoned, at least as far as the Mississippi River, probably to a base in the Deep South.

We were assigned berth numbers on boarding, and I was elated to draw a lower. But my elation was short-lived. A big, rawboned kid seated next to me explained that two men were assigned to each lower berth, and he would be my bunkmate.

The window shades had been pulled down and we were warned of dire punishment if anyone dared to raise them. Not until next morning could we look out to check the names of the stations we passed. Surprisingly, the lower berth was roomy enough for two, but in my excitement, I slept very little. Thursday at dawn a noncom came through the car shouting the litany we were to hear many times: "Awright, it's reveille time! Drop yer cocks an' grab yer socks!"

While I waited in line for the toilet, I looked out at a passing cornfield. "Kansas, right?" I asked the black porter.

"Naw suh," he replied. "Nebraska. Y'all gonna get off fo' breakfast at Hastings."

Sure enough, at about seven that morning the train slowed to a stop across from an old station bearing the sign HASTINGS under its clock. We had come more than halfway across the state of Nebraska.

Two or three MPs stood on the platform, and a few old farmers in straw hats watched us get off and form up facing the noncoms who passed out breakfast chits. A sergeant pointed at two cafés.

"Yer chits are good fer fifty cents at either o' them two joints," he said. "This here train leaves in an hour at eight sharp. Any of ya big spenders wants t' spend his own dough an' take his chances on missin' the train, there's a bigger place a coupla

BREAKFAST STOP AT HASTINGS, NEBRASKA

blocks down that street. Next chow won't be till ya git where yer goin'. Better shag ass! DeTAIL disMISSED!"

Stan Detrick, Gordon Bungaard, and I had agreed to stick together, and when we saw the crowd of hungry recruits shoving its way into the two small cafés, we decided to try the bigger place. We were the only "big spenders" who took the chance. If the sergeant was not kidding about no more chow until we arrived at our final destination, we thought, we might not eat again until the next morning! It did not occur to any of us that we would reach our destination before noon.

All I remember of that breakfast in Hastings was my nervous impatience with the slow waitress; with Bungaard, who took his time eating; and with Detrick, who laughed every time we heard a steam whistle and I looked at my watch in panic. We finally got our checks, paid in a rush, and ran like hell back to the train with me in the lead, gasping, "C'mon, we're gonna miss it!" But we made it in plenty of time.

Back in my seat, I looked at my railroad map and saw that the tracks went east from Hastings to the state capital at Lincoln. I took the map of army bases from my wallet, and lo!, there I found Lincoln Army Air Base, northwest of the city. I bet my seatmate a quarter that was our destination.

Sure enough, well before noon we unloaded in the shimmering heat of Lincoln, and I won my quarter. A detail of sweating recruits was sent forward to the baggage car to throw down our barracks bags where several Army Air Corps buses waited in the sun. The buses were like ovens, and even with all windows open our new suntan uniforms were soon soaked with sweat.

Miserable with thirst, we arrived at Lincoln Army Air Base just before noon and were lined up facing a leathery, white-haired old sergeant in a safari-type sun helmet. He informed us in a deep southern drawl that we were now in Flight 53 of the U.S. Army Air Corps' 604th Training Group. The word "flight" was music to my would-be pilot's ears. In the distance I could see hangars and concrete runways, where twin-engine C-47 transports were taking off and landing as we marched off to shabbily constructed barracks covered with tar paper—a far cry from the neat white barracks at Fort Logan.

Inside the hot barracks we chose our bunks, and there was a rush for the single water fountain, where a corporal handed two salt tablets to each man in the slow-moving line, making sure we swallowed them to avoid heat prostration. Then we marched to noon chow at the mess hall, where the main course was creamed chipped beef on toast, known to millions of uniformed Americans in World War II as SOS or Shit on a Shingle.

That afternoon we were issued field gear, including a raincoat, plastic helmet liner, canteen, mess kit, wraparound canvas leggings, two pairs of rough leather half boots, and a gas mask. Then we marched off for a series of IQ and mechanical aptitude tests. An officer explained that only those who scored at least 110 on the IQ test, met certain other standards, and passed the physical and eye exams might apply for flight training. Furthermore, any would-be pilot who screwed up during basic training would be automatically disqualified.

TAKING IQ AND MECHANICAL APTITUDE TESTS

The officer, who wore thick glasses, explained that those who met all requirements except the eye test might apply to Air Corps Officer Candidate School (OCS) and be commissioned as an aerial navigator or bombardier, or for a nonflying job such as his. Barring that, he enumerated a list of noncommissioned options including aerial gunner, radioman, and photographer (for which the eyesight requirements were less stringent), or ground jobs such as meteorologist, aircraft mechanic, and armorer. As I knew my eyes were 20-40 without glasses, I had given up all hope of becoming a pilot but was consoled to think that I might yet become a flying navigator or bombardier.

It turned out that the eye tests eliminated me from flying in any capacity, and in the first letters I wrote home from Lincoln Army Air Base I tried hard to hide my disappointment. Then, in a letter written on Friday, July 16, there was one bright note: I and eighteen others of the two hundred in Flight 53 had, on the basis of IQ and education, been selected to apply for something called the Army Specialized Training Program, or ASTP. This program would send us back to college to complete our education in either engineering, foreign languages, psychology, or premed.

I cautioned my parents that only half of the eighteen would be accepted into the ASTP, but that those who were not might still apply for the Air Corps OCS. A week later, three days after my nineteenth birthday, I wrote elatedly that I had been accepted! Barring an unforeseen development, I would be sent to some college to study engineering in the fall, following basic training. In two years, with luck, I would have a degree and become an "officer and a gentleman" in the U.S. Army Corps of Engineers, or the Air Corps, or some other technical branch— not the dreaded infantry, thank God. Little did I know.

After the pleasant surprise of having qualified for ASTP I remember secretly hoping that basic training would be tough. This hope stemmed from my need to prove myself a real soldier before going back to the soft life of college, and from there, I assumed, to some relatively safe rear-echelon job for the duration of the war. But in hindsight, except for heat, humidity, and poor food, the Air Corps basic training was almost a joke compared to the infantry training I would go through later in 1944.

One afternoon several hundred recruits who had eaten the

day-old bread pudding served at lunch were suddenly struck with ptomaine poisoning and sent to the base hospital in ambulances. I was one of them. That was by far my worst experience during Air Corps basic training, and I swore never again to eat bread pudding. I have to this day, more than half a century later, kept that vow.

August came, and Flight 53 had yet to see its first rifle, pistol, hand grenade, or bayonet close up. As yet we had spent no nights out in the rain or in foxholes, nor made any long hikes with full field gear. Not until the seventh week of basic were we at last issued full field gear and sent to a remote former National Guard camp, where we lived in tents, learned to dig foxholes, ate canned C rations, made a few night marches, and crawled through an infiltration course under live fire. Then we were taken to a firing range, where we fired the new army carbine, the Thompson submachine gun, and the .45-caliber automatic pistol. I qualified as a marksman with the carbine and submachine gun but did poorly with the pistol.

Given a Sunday pass after returning from the outing in the field, I joined Detrick, Bungaard, and a new friend named Buell Moore on a bus to the Nebraska State Fair. As we were about to leave the boring displays of farm equipment and 4-H exhibits, we spotted a tent with a sign proclaiming "Nude Dancing Girls." Never before having seen an adult nude female in the flesh, I decided it was time to rectify this shortcoming in my education. For fifty cents each, my buddies and I joined the group of old farmers ogling an ugly middle-aged woman and a pathetic young girl—probably her daughter—as they pranced around nude and did a few bumps and grinds to the accompaniment of a scratchy phonograph record. To me the performance was more disgusting than sexy, but at least my youthful curiosity had been satisfied.

Later, Bungaard and Detrick went off to find some beer while Buell Moore and I, both teetotalers, took the next bus to downtown Lincoln and spent the rest of the day sight-seeing.

SUNDAY VISIT TO THE NEBRASKA STATE FAIR

Basic was over on September 3, 1943. In my last letter from Lincoln Army Air Base I told of a Flight 53 party at the All-American Café in Lincoln, and wrote piously: "We nondrinkers put the drunks under the shower, and then to bed."

A week later those of us selected for ASTP were bused to the campus of Nebraska University's Agricultural College to take more tests before our final acceptance into the program. I was required to take a two-week refresher course in physics before I was finally shipped out, with five others, to ASTP Unit 3926 at the University of Idaho, in the college town of Moscow.

CHAPTER 3

THE ASTP AT MOSCOW

October 1943 to March 1944

Stan Detrick was the only one I knew in the small group that was sent from the U.S. Army Air Corps to the ASTP unit at the University of Idaho, so the two of us stuck together. The two-day trip began with a short bus ride to Fremont, Nebraska, where we boarded a Union Pacific passenger train. This train took us across southern Wyoming and Idaho to Pendleton, Oregon. There, at 1:00 A.M. on Monday, October 4, 1943, we boarded a second train, which took us to Walla Walla, Washington. And finally, at 5:00 A.M., we transferred to an ancient local train, which brought us to Moscow, where we arrived sometime before noon.

Classes did not begin until the following Monday, October 11, so there was little to do for a week. After registering, we settled into the men's dorm taken over by the ASTP, checked out our textbooks, explored the town, played Ping-Pong at the USO, and met some coeds. In the first letter I wrote home from Moscow, I said that the girls were unexpectedly friendly, and explained their friendliness by saying that the civilian male student population is almost nil, and that they considered us to be college students, a supposedly higher type of army specimen.

Today, six decades later, I can't recall any names or faces of the girls at the University of Idaho. In fact, with the exception of two "dates" I had taken to the movies during high school, there had been no girls in my life—nor would there be until just after the war in Europe ended in May 1945, two months before my twenty-first birthday.

We soldier-students were warned that we would be sent back to the *real army* if our grades fell below a B average. I for one learned to study as if my very life depended on it during that fall and winter quarter of 1943–44. I became a near straight-A student, falling short only with a B-plus in history.

We wore a diamond-shaped ASTP shoulder patch with a blue lamp and flame superimposed on a blue sword against a yellow background. Although we wore uniforms, marched to and from classes and the mess hall, had five hours of "military" each week, were supposed to study at specific times each evening until lights out, and were at times called out for parades or an hour of close-order drill, we were more student than soldier. We considered ourselves lucky. There was no KP duty, except as punishment for some infraction of the rules. Civilian women ran the mess hall, and coeds did the serving.

Shortly after our arrival, there was a shuffle in platoon and room assignments. Detrick was sent to a different platoon, and I found myself with three new roommates—Bill Lueck from Toledo, H. K. Eddington from some town in eastern Idaho, and Steve Longo from New Orleans. Our courses that first term included analytic geometry, physics, chemistry, English, geography, American history, physical training (primarily swimming), and "military."

There was surprisingly little snow in Moscow that fall—just rain, wind, and mud. Most of my spare time was spent writing letters, playing Ping-Pong, or joining my new roommates at the downtown movie on Saturday nights.

Mother sent me box after box of candy and cookies, which I was glad to share with my three roommates. Lueck's mother sent Thuringer sausage, Eddington's sent cakes and pies, and Longo's sent jars of Italian antipasto.

In mid-November a young private was caught with more than a hundred dollars' worth of watches, pens, cigarette lighters, and money stolen from several study rooms in the dorm. One of the watches was mine, with my initials engraved on it. As a result, six other students and I were sent up to Spokane, Washington, as witnesses at the thief's general court-martial. The trial was postponed from Wednesday the twenty-fourth to Saturday the twenty-seventh, so we were there for four days, including Thanksgiving dinner, and did not arrive back in Moscow until Sunday. Fortunately, the ASTP commandant asked our professors to go easy on us; hence our grades didn't suffer from the fact that we missed two days of classes and had to make up one or two tests.

There were to be no furloughs until after the first quarter ended on Thursday, December 30. I remember Christmas 1943 as the loneliest day of my life up to that time. Not only was the bleak, snowless landscape around Moscow depressing, but also rumor had it that the ASTP would be abolished in March and we would all be sent to the infantry. We were offered a two-day pass over Christmas, but to save money for my upcoming furlough I stayed in Moscow, ate Christmas dinner in the half-empty mess hall, and studied hard for the first quarter's finals, hoping against hope that the rumor was false.

At last, on New Year's Day 1944, I headed home for my first leave. Of those ten precious days, six were spent coming and going, and four in the warm cocoon of my parents' home. My pal Jeff came over, and we listened to classical music on the record player, but it was a somewhat somber reunion, as Jeff was a 4-F civilian whose poor eyesight had kept him out of the service. Our other two pals had just been drafted and were gone—Bill Powell to the navy, and Leon Ayedelotte to the navy's Seabees—an acronym for CB or Construction Battalion.

My return trip to Idaho was uneventful except for a long delay in the frigid town of Green River, Wyoming, which resulted in a missed train connection. A bit of good news awaited me on my return to Moscow. My grade average for the first quarter was close to 4.0, and I was one of three in the unit to receive special orders permitting us to wear, as an award, the ASTP Blue Star of Scholastic Excellence. And the three of us took turns marching our platoon to class. Maybe, I thought, this would

HONOR STUDENT MARCHING THE GROUP TO CLASS

keep me out of the infantry if the rumored abolishment of the ASTP turned out to be true. Or perhaps I could still apply for the Army Air Corps OCS and become an officer and a gentleman.

One Friday in mid-February 1944 it finally snowed in earnest, and the girls of several sororities challenged the ASTP to a snowball fight. Writing of this battle, which began in a tennis court and soon spread into the street in front of the sorority houses, I said: "The girls proved to be better shots than we thought, and we were outnumbered so terrifically that we got beat up pretty badly. Many of the girls are little demons in a snow fight."

Ah, what innocent fun that was! One of my few carefree memories of the ASTP was that of a very pretty girl who sat on me and stuffed snow down my neck. Oh, how I wanted to get to know her and ask her out on a date! But I was far too shy.

Toward the end of February 1944 the rumored abolishment of the ASTP at the end of March became fact, and it was announced that most of the men in ASTP Unit 3926 would be sent to the infantry. My letters home were for the most part cheerful, hiding my great disappointment and fear for what my future would bring.

In mid-1942, when the ASTP had been established, it was expected that the war would last through 1946 at least. And it was widely believed that the key to victory lay in technology and mass production of modern weapons of war—aircraft, tanks, and ships—as opposed to huge invasion armies of infantrymen. The idea of the ASTP was to pick a select group of draftees with a year or two of college, accelerate their education in critical specialties, and place them in technical branches of the army, such as Ordnance, the Corps of Engineers, and the Signal Corps.

But in March 1944 General Eisenhower—by then in England planning the invasion of France—decided that he needed another two hundred thousand combat troops to assure a successful invasion and the subsequent defeat of Nazi Germany. And lo, there just happened to be, almost to the exact round number, two hundred thousand young Americans in the ASTP, few of whom would complete the equivalent of four years of college before 1945—probably too late to make a difference. The bloody invasions of Sicily and Italy had convinced Ike that victory depended on the poor bloody infantry after all—in large numbers.

Those of us in the ASTP were not alone in our misery at being so suddenly selected to become cannon fodder. By this time the Army Air Corps had more student pilots than it could possibly use. And so the fateful decision that sent me to the infantry, along with most of the two hundred thousand student-soldiers in the ASTP, also applied to several thousand bitter Army Air Corps cadets. Small consolation, I thought, but had my eyes qualified me to fly, I might nevertheless have been one of that sad group who were sent to the infantry from the Army Air Corps.

On March 24, after the last and now meaningless ASTP "finals" were finished, I joined several others in serenading the sorority girls who lived across the street from our dorm. Then, the next day, there was an unmemorable "graduation" ceremony. And the day after that it was announced that all but a few of us would be sent to the 71st Light Infantry Division at a place in California called the Hunter-Liggett Military Reservation, about forty miles south of Monterey.

Late Wednesday afternoon, March 29, 1944, as a band played and coeds waved good-bye, the troop train for Hunter-Liggett left Moscow, Idaho. And so ended my dream of avoiding the dreaded infantry. It was a bitter pill. Like thousands of others, I had begun to think of myself as one of the elite. *You should have known it was too good to be true,* I said to myself. *If you had stayed in the Army Air Corps you'd at least be wearing the sergeant's stripes of an aircraft mechanic by now.*

CHAPTER 4

HUNTER-LIGGETT MILITARY RESERVATION

April and May 1944

I had never traveled as far west as California, so I found the train trip down to Hunter-Liggett especially exciting. I stared in awe at the Columbia River; at baby flattops in the harbor at Portland, Oregon; at the snowcapped peak of Mount Hood; at the giant redwood trees of southern Oregon and northern California; and at a vast armada of ships in the bay west of Oakland. But I was disappointed that the San Francisco skyline and the fabled Golden Gate Bridge were invisible in the fog over the bay.

South of Oakland the rain-soaked hills were green, and when we passed lush fruit orchards and vineyards and towns with Spanish names, I felt as if we were entering a strange and exotic land of plenty, softer and more feminine than the Rocky Mountain states. And I almost expected to hear vaqueros serenading pretty señoritas to the accompaniment of guitars, as in the movies.

Our rail journey ended at Camp Roberts, rear base of the 71st Light Infantry Division. There we were issued steel helmets, mess kits, packs, blankets, and raincoats. The next day a truck convoy brought us to a tent camp in the rugged foothills of the coastal range west of King City, not far from William Randolph Hearst's famous castle at San Simeon. It was in those mountains that the experimental 71st was engaged in maneuvers against the 89th Infantry Division.

The 71st had been formed in Colorado in mid-1943 by combining three infantry regiments: the 5th, 14th, and 66th. All of us from the ASTP were sent to the 5th Infantry. How ironic, I thought, remembering from newspaper stories that this regiment was the same mule-equipped outfit my father and I had seen near Camp Carson ten months earlier, headed for Pike's Peak, and I had vowed then and there *never* to become a foot soldier if I could possibly help it.

At the base camp we were told that the experimental 71st had "three thousand mules and one jeep for the general." It was said that after the maneuvers were over, the army planned to send the 71st Division to join the ragtag army in Burma commanded by General "Vinegar Joe" Stilwell. This, and the fact that we were issued jungle-style packs, led some to refer to it as a "jungle division."

I dreaded the thought of fighting Japanese in the jungle. Given a choice, if I had to be an infantryman, I much preferred to be sent to fight in Europe, where at least there was some civilization and the German enemy was reputedly more humane.

It was also said that two other divisions would join us in Burma—the 89th, which had a combination of mules and trucks, and the 10th Mountain Division, made up primarily of ski troops. But as it turned out, none of these three divisions went to Stilwell's army. All three were sent to Eisenhower in Europe.

At Hunter-Liggett I was initially assigned to Battery D of a 75mm pack artillery battalion, and for several days I learned how to rig pack saddles and load mountain howitzers on the backs of balky mules. Eight of us newcomers lived in a pyramid tent, in a valley surrounded by steep mountains. We subsisted on our first C rations—two cans per man for each meal. One can always had some kind of meat, and the other had crackers and a packet of instant coffee, or cocoa, or lemonade.

Easter Sunday brought a respite from C rations, and I dutifully attended the Protestant church services held in a large open field. But the hot meal served by the field kitchen after the services was a far cry from the Easter banquets my mother used to prepare.

The newcomers from the ASTP and the Air Corps were not yet active participants in the maneuvers going on in the higher mountains. But to get us in shape, our noncoms subjected us to daily hikes up the firebreak trails, carrying heavy jungle packs or

PACK ARTILLERY MULE SKINNERS IN TRAINING

pushing and pulling two-wheeled carts loaded with rocks. Even so, I decided I was lucky to be a muleskinner in the pack artillery rather than a front-line infantryman. But even that was not to last. A week later, several of us were unceremoniously transferred to G Company of the 5th Infantry Regiment. And so I became a lowly infantry "dogface" after all.

We were told that this transfer was part of a major reorganization resulting from the fact that the maneuvers had been unexpectedly cut short after nearly a month of heavy rain, most of which had fallen before we arrived. The resulting floods and swollen mountain streams caused the drowning of many mules and some men, and made the supply of the troops up on the peaks next to impossible. The following extracts from my *History of the U.S. Army 71st Infantry Division*, published in June 1945 after the war ended in Europe, tell the story:

> Then the famous 21 days of the 71st Light Division began. There haven't been 21 days like it since, not even in combat, and to hear the men talk about it, one wonders how even one man survived it.
>
> As the Division reached farther into the mountains and farther away from the main supply base, the supply problem became more complicated. Food had almost disappeared. The rains came again, coupled with an incessant wind. Casualties from colds, poison oak, and exhaustion again began to mount. These maneuvers had been officially pronounced the toughest ever held by the Army, and they were taking their toll. At one time over 1500 men were hospitalized.

I saw some of these casualties one morning as a half-blind squad of men, their eyes puffed shut from poison oak, were led down the firebreak trail past the base camp. Later that day a jeep roared down the mountain and its occupants shouted, "The war's over!"

By that night it was official: The maneuvers ended before any of us new men had seen the crest of those steep mountains overlooking the Pacific. The next day it was learned that most of the "old-timer" privates who had been with the regiments that made up the 71st even before it was activated would be sent to the China-Burma-India (CBI) Theater, along with a few thousand mules. The noncoms would, however, stay with us as a cadre around which we newcomers would be reorganized and retrained as a "standard" infantry division.

The rumor was that we would be sent to Fort Leonard Wood in Missouri, or Camp A. P. Hill in Virginia, or Fort Bragg in North Carolina. There was no mention of Fort Benning, Georgia, where the remnants of the division were in fact sent a month later, after four thousand old-timers were sent to the CBI.

For some reason military organization charts have always fascinated me—perhaps because they tell a story of how the chain of command is structured, and paint a picture of how all the "parts" fit and work together, like a machine. In any case, I wrote a long letter home explaining how the 71st Infantry Division was organized, from the commanding general and his staff all the way down to the sergeants who led the squads. I named and described the three subordinate infantry regiments, the three infantry battalions per regiment, the three rifle companies and one heavy weapons company per infantry battalion, and on down to the platoon and squad levels within each company.

I suspect that this organizational description must have bored my parents. Suffice it to say that I was in G Company of the 2d Battalion, 5th Infantry Regiment, and that this company, like all standard infantry companies in World War II, fielded six officers and 180 enlisted men organized into five platoons.

The headquarters platoon included the company commander, Capt. Herbert Neil; the company executive officer, First Lieutenant Doneski; 1st Sgt. Carl Anderson; and thirty others, including two clerks, a bugler, a communications section, a supply section, a mess section, a security squad, drivers, and medics attached from the battalion medical section.

Captain Neil was a six-foot, four-inch giant from Arizona. It was said that he had been in the army since he was sixteen. First Sergeant Anderson, G Company's "topkick," was a grimy-looking Maine fisherman, respectfully called "Top" to his face but known behind his back as "The Grimy One."

The company had three rifle platoons, numbered the 1st, 2d, and 3d. Each of these was led by a second lieutenant, assisted by a platoon sergeant (technical sergeant), a platoon guide (staff sergeant), and a platoon runner. Each rifle platoon had three rifle squads, each led by a staff sergeant.

The fourth platoon of each rifle company was known as the weapons platoon. It was led by a second lieutenant, assisted by a platoon sergeant (technical sergeant) and a runner. This platoon was made up of a light .30-caliber machine gun section and a light 60mm mortar section, each led by a staff sergeant. The machine gun section had two machine guns (two squads, five men per squad), with a sergeant in command of each squad. The mortar section had three mortars (three squads, five men per squad), with a sergeant in command of each squad.

The 71st Infantry Division commander at the time was Major General Spragins, who would be replaced later by Maj. Gen. Willard G. Wyman. The 5th Infantry Regiment was commanded by Col. Sidney C. Wooten. Its 2d Battalion was commanded by Lt. Col. Charles M. Gettys.

A few days after the maneuvers ended, Colonel Wooten briefed the new men on the history of the 5th Infantry Regiment. I was fascinated to learn that the regiment was actually the third oldest infantry regiment in the U.S. Army. It was designated as the 5th rather than the 3d because during the War of 1812 each new regiment was numbered according to the date of rank of its first commander, and its colonel at the time it was formed was one James Miller, who ranked fifth in the army.

Colonel Wooten went on to explain that the regimental motto—"I'll try, sir"—was derived from an incident at a place in upstate New York called Lundy's Lane, during an all-day battle with the British in 1814. It seems that several other regiments had been repeatedly repulsed when trying to capture a hill defended by seven British cannons. The American general in overall command, one Jacob Brown, asked Colonel Miller "Sir, can your regiment clear those guns off that hill?" Miller replied, "I'll try, sir," proceeded to take the hill with his men, and so the 5th Infantry's motto was born.

The regiment was with General Zachary Taylor's army in Mexico in 1847, where it helped capture the fortress of Chapultepec. Then it returned to New Mexico and Texas to guard frontier settlements against the Navajo and Apache tribes. In 1857 it was sent to Florida to fight the Seminoles, then to Utah to fight the Mormons. But it saw little action during the Civil War, as it remained stationed out West.

In 1874 the regiment helped defeat the Kiowas and Comanches under Chief Satanta, and had a major role in forcing the surrender of Sitting Bull and Crazy Horse after "Custer's Last Stand" in 1876 at the Little Big Horn in Montana. A few years later it participated in the chase and capture of Chief Joseph's heroic Nez Pierce tribe in Montana, and until 1888 it patrolled the northern frontier in North Dakota and Montana.

During the Spanish-American War the regiment served briefly in Cuba, then was sent to the Philippines in 1900 to quell a Moro uprising. Until 1914 it divided its time between Plattsburgh Barracks, New York, and Cuba. Then at the start of World War I it was sent to guard the Panama Canal, and then to Louisiana in 1918. After a few years on occupation duty in the German Rhineland, it settled down for a long stint of garrison duty in Maine. Then, in 1939, when World War II broke out in Europe, the regiment was again sent back to guard the Panama

Canal. Finally, in 1943, it arrived at Camp Carson, Colorado, and was made part of the new 71st Infantry Division.

On a rainy April day in 1944, while several of us were digging a latrine trench, a sergeant announced that anyone who had not had a furlough for the past ninety days would be offered eleven days' leave starting at six that night. Although I was almost broke and would have to call home for the round-trip train fare to Denver, I jumped at the chance. Four of us from Colorado ran to the single phone booth that stood incongruously in the rain by the road to the camp.

We waited in line, called our homes, and as no buses ran from the reservation to the nearest rail line at King City, we called for a taxicab to pick us up at six. But that second leave started off badly for me.

By six that night it was raining hard and I was late getting my rifle cleaned and bringing it and my two duffel bags to the supply tent for storage. The tent was dark, but a light showed through the flap of the adjacent headquarters tent, and I could hear voices. I didn't want to set my heavy bags down in the mud, so I stupidly threw one of them through the headquarters tent flap. Oh, boy, did old Top ever chew me out—while Captain Neal turned his back and laughed silently.

"Private Joy," Anderson said, "You are the *worst an' sorriest* goddamn sojer I ever did see! I got a good mind t'cancel yer leave and put ya on KP. When ya enter this tent ya knock first, salute the cap'n, say '*Yessir,*' '*Nosir,*' an' that's it. Now git the hell outta here!"

I don't recall how I managed to get my gear and rifle into the supply tent, but in any case the taxi had come and gone while I was being chewed out. I swallowed my anger, found another tardy GI to share a cab, and after a long, miserable wait in the rain by the phone booth, another cab came. By the time we arrived at King City, the 10:00 P.M. train for San Francisco had come and gone. Luckily, at about 1:00 A.M., another northbound train came along. But it was nearly dawn by the time it pulled into San Francisco's Third Street railroad station.

My companion left for someplace on a bus, and I found myself alone in the foggy city, with no place to sleep. I wandered the streets until 8:00 A.M., when the Western Union office on Market Street opened and I could get the money my father had wired from Denver. I walked past sleeping winos, scared out of my wits that I'd be robbed of my last few dollars. With nothing better to do, I walked to the San Francisco–Oakland Bay Bridge without incident, and by 8:00 A.M. was back at the Western Union office, tired but relieved to get fifty dollars to put into my wallet.

I ate a lonely breakfast of ham and eggs at a cheap diner, got a haircut, then walked to the Ferry Building and met the three Colorado boys who had left me in the lurch. Late that afternoon we finally had our tickets, crossed the bay to Oakland on the ferry, and boarded our train to Denver.

One afternoon during my second furlough, a friend from high school days named Al Bragg showed up at the door wearing the uniform of a Marine Corps second lieutenant, including pilot wings. He had joined the Marines in the fall of 1942 when Jeff and I had gone to college at the University of Colorado. Now he was a brand-new F4U Corsair fighter pilot, and I was still a lowly private without so much as a single stripe on my sleeve. I fought to keep my jealousy from showing, found it hard to be gracious, but managed to say, "Gee, Al, congratulations. But I hope you don't expect me to salute you?"

"Nah, of course not," Al laughed. The reunion was mercifully short, and I was glad when he left. Somehow that episode has stuck in my mind for all these years, erasing whatever other memories I might have retained from that second furlough.

The first letter I wrote home after returning to Hunter-Liggett describes only the trouble I had getting back to camp from San Francisco. A sold-out train; a canceled Greyhound bus;

then a rush back to the train depot to take a later train, which didn't arrive in King City until just before midnight. Several of us who had missed our connections had the foresight to get an MP's note to the effect that our train had been late and the bus had been canceled. Nothing was said when I checked in at G Company two hours late.

The next day it was announced that the remnants of the 71st Light Infantry Division were to ship out to Fort Benning, Georgia, for reorganization and retraining as a "standard" (as opposed to "light") infantry division.

That night I was on guard duty, from 2:00 A.M. to 4:00 A.M., with the assignment of patrolling up and down our muddy "street" between two long rows of tents. I was issued *no ammunition* for my M1 rifle—probably because I had never yet fired that weapon. During Air Corps basic we had fired only the light carbine and the .45-caliber pistol.

One of my assignments as guard was to check the last tent every time I came to the end of the street, to be sure that a young private sharing that tent with the company bugler had not run away. It seems he was under company arrest for being AWOL, and would be court-martialed the next day. Whoever set up that guard detail didn't plan very well. It turned out that each of us had to walk back up to a tent near company headquarters when our shift was up and wake the sergeant of the guard, who was supposed to be awake. And so, when the man who took over my shift checked the tent in which the culprit private was supposed to be, he was gone—and so was the bugler!

The captain and the sergeant of the guard called all of us into the headquarters tent after learning of this, and everyone concluded that the two men must have left at the end of my shift, when I was walking back to wake up the sergeant. For a few minutes I thought I was in serious trouble. But it was the sergeant who got chewed out for having been asleep and making us come wake *him* up to be relieved. I often wondered what I was supposed to do had I, armed as I was with an empty rifle, actually *seen* the men escape and challenged them to halt.

On a Sunday in mid-May, a week before we boarded the troop trains for Georgia, a group of Hollywood actors put on an outdoor show on a makeshift stage in a large clearing. The emcee was George Murphy, and with him came two actresses, Carole Landis and Virginia Belmont; a model turned actress named Chili Williams; two other starlets; and a girl named Rosemary LaPlanche, who had been Miss America of 1941.

Murphy cracked dirty jokes as Chili and the other starlets strode across the stage in bathing suits. Carole Landis sang a few songs. And toward the end of the show she called for jitterbug volunteers. The two GIs who jitterbugged with her were rewarded with long, passionate kisses as several thousand sex-starved GIs whistled and moaned.

My battalion left Hunter-Liggett on a Saturday afternoon, May 20, 1944. It took five days for the troop train to cross Arizona, New Mexico, southeastern Colorado, Kansas, Missouri, southern Illinois, western Kentucky and Tennessee, the northeastern corner of Mississippi, then across central Alabama to Birmingham and on to Columbus, Georgia, a few miles west of Fort Benning.

CHAPTER 5

FORT BENNING

May 25, 1944, to January 11, 1945

Fort Benning, Georgia, was then, as it is today, the home of the U.S. Army Infantry School. It was there in a chigger-infested training area called Sand Hill that the reorganized 71st Infantry Division would slowly fill its ranks and spend the next thirty-five weeks—instead of the normal twenty-four—learning the bloody trade of the infantry before being shipped to France.

One of my pals who joined G Company at Fort Benning was a likable kid named Kenny Stevens. We soon became good friends, but since he had already completed some months of infantry training in a different division, he was suddenly sent overseas as an infantry replacement not long after the D-day invasion of France on June 6, 1944. Weeks later, I received a letter from Kenny, written from a hospital in England, with the news that he had been wounded on his very first day in combat! Lonely as I was after he left, I imagined *nothing* could be worse than being sent up to the front as a green replacement and joining a strange outfit where you knew no one.

I think the army's replacement policy back then was stupid. How many times I have read of the high casualties suffered by new infantry replacements who never even got to know their sergeant's name before being killed or wounded on their first day of combat. Those of us who stayed with the 71st and survived the war were lucky. Not only did we miss D-day, we also missed the bloody Battle of the Bulge in the cold Ardennes the following December. But our sixty days in combat were bloody enough.

Although my spirits were low that June, the letters I wrote home don't show it. They were full of bravado and attempts at humor. I drew detailed sketches of infantry weapons and maps of tactical exercises. Today I recognize that this was an attempt to boost my spirits and self-esteem by showing how much I knew about my new profession, even though I was still a lowly buck private. It was not until two weeks before my twentieth birthday that I was finally given the single stripe of a pfc. But the extra four dollars per month in pay did little to raise my spirits.

There was not much hope of early promotion to corporal or buck sergeant, as G Company was overloaded with these ranks. This was primarily because of the recent arrival of several ex-air cadets transferred from the Army Air Corps. Most of them wore stripes, and this quickly filled G Company's available NCO slots. Although most of these newcomers were a year or two older than I was, I resented their stripes. On marches we used to sing a parody of a popular Army Air Corps song that reflects this resentment. Here are the first two lines of the proper lyrics:

Into the air, Army Air Corps, into the Air, pilots true. Into the air, Army Air Corps, keep your nose up in the blue, up in the blue.

The parody went like this:

> Into the air, junior birdmen, into the air, oh, you clowns.
> Into the air, junior birdmen, keep your nose up in the
> brown, up in the brown, and when you hear the grand
> announcement, that you'll get your wings of tin, you can
> bet the junior birdmen will send their box tops in—it
> takes but four.

In the last week of July I was transferred from a rifle platoon to G Company's 4th Platoon, better known as the weapons platoon, and assigned as acting gunner in the 3d Squad of the 60mm mortar section. My squad leader was Sgt. John Rohan, from Racine, Wisconsin, and he and I were to become good friends. In fact, he would be the only one from G Company I would stay in touch with after the war.

A few weeks after this change, a sergeant named Cirillo and I were the only ones in the mortar section who qualified as expert with the 60mm mortar, so I became officially the 3d squad's gunner under Johnny Rohan.

Our platoon leader was 2d Lt. Joseph Tyler, and our platoon sergeant was TSgt. Alfred Feltman. The machine gun section of two squads was led by SSgt. Henry Rodewald, and our mortar section of three squads was led by SSgt. Morton Cree.

The 1st Mortar Squad was led by Sergeant Cirillo, and the 2d by Sgt. H. K. Bailey. In my squad, led by Sergeant Rohan with me as his gunner, I had an assistant gunner named Glen Decker, and two ammunition bearers named Waitus Hatley and Roland Vincent.

Training at Benning included throwing live hand grenades; assaulting mocked-up towns and bunkers; firing the antitank bazooka; long road marches (some at night); and several night patrols that usually ended up at the dreaded infiltration course, where we crawled through barbed wire under live machine-gun fire as dynamite or TNT exploded nearby.

In addition to training in the field, there were morning calisthenics, running the obstacle course, KP duty once or twice a month, and scrubbing barracks for Saturday morning inspection. And, of course, every afternoon at about five we fell in for

CAPTAIN NEAL INSPECTS RIFLES

inspection, usually by Captain Neal, with First Sergeant Anderson ("The Grimy One") following just behind him.

Once I was on a guard detail at Fort Benning's Main Post, keeping watch over several hardcase stockade prisoners as they picked up trash along the roads. Sundays were usually free, but one Sunday morning I was assigned to a detail that cleaned up the Officers' Club after a Saturday night party.

It took us hours to clean the place up, then mop and wax the dance floor. As I was still a righteous teetotaler and nonsmoker, the job of emptying ashtrays and gathering half-empty lipstick-smeared cocktail glasses reeking of stale booze and soggy cigarette butts particularly disgusted me. "Why can't those drunken officers and their wives or girlfriends clean up their own mess?" I fumed.

My recreation at Benning was limited to drinking Cokes at the PX, attending on-post movies, hitchhiking to the Main Post to write letters at the Enlisted Men's Club or to watch the paratroopers jump from their training towers, and a few Sunday trips to the town of Columbus for a steak or southern fried chicken dinner. Only once did two of my teetotaler friends and I cross the Chattahoochee River to the Alabama town of Phenix City—said to be a real den of iniquity, full of thieves and whores. We steered clear of the roughest part of town, took a cab to a riding stable, rented horses for a few hours, then came back across the river before dark.

By the end of September the 71st Infantry Division was approaching full strength, and we were told that it would soon be ready for the final field exercises to determine if we were ready for combat. By October it seemed certain that we would be sent to fight the Germans in Europe if the war lasted long enough. Familiarization with German weapons, uniforms, and organization—rather than Japanese—was the clue.

My platoon sergeant, TSgt Alfred Feltman, was a naturalized U.S. citizen who had been born in Germany. He had deserted from the German army in 1939 and made his way to New York to join his parents. In exchange for immediate U.S. citizenship he had joined the U.S. Army, and was one of the NCOs singled out at Benning to demonstrate German arms, uniforms, and close-order drill. I was elated when Feltman chose me to join his ten-man demonstration squad. They dressed me in a captured German private's uniform complete with Mauser rifle, coal-scuttle helmet, and a belt with a buckle engraved with the words *Gott mit Uns* (God with Us).

Feltman, wearing the uniform of a German *Feldwebel* (platoon sergeant), put our squad through its paces in front of the entire 2d Battalion of the 5th Infantry Regiment. His act included snarling German curses, spitting in the face of one of the squad members who dropped his rifle in the dirt, then striking him a blow and knocking his helmet off. I enjoyed every minute of my role as a hated Kraut. The show was so successful it was repeated for the other two battalions of the regiment.

FELTMAN'S MOCK GERMAN DEMONSTRATION SQUAD

On October 13 the division was alerted for overseas movement, and packing began. Then the alert was called off, the move was rescheduled for sometime in November, and several members of G Company—myself included—were given two-week furloughs starting on Saturday, October 14, 1944.

That last furlough to Denver began with an unforgettable episode at the Columbus depot, where hundreds of Fort Benning GIs were sleeping on newspapers spread on the floor to keep from getting their uniforms dirty as they waited for their trains to depart. Dressed in clean, well-pressed suntans, I found an abandoned newspaper and spread it on a vacant spot where I could stretch out for an hour or so before my train time. I had just fallen asleep when I felt a sharp kick in my ribs and heard an angry voice saying, "Goddamn, you no steal my place!" I felt a second kick and looked up to see a drunk little Mexican-American GI with smoldering dark eyes.

I was never by nature much of a fighter, but with that I gathered all the courage I could summon and said, "You kick me again and I'll get up and beat the shit out of you!"

But the angry aggressor, who could not have been more than five and a half feet tall and probably weighed no more than 125 pounds, aimed another kick, which missed as I rolled and stood up with my fists clenched. And with that *he pulled a knife!*

I was by then five feet, ten inches tall and weighed 145 pounds. The sight of that blade caused my rage to overcome my natural fear. I dodged as the knife-wielding Mexican lunged and missed, then I struck him a smashing blow full in the face, knocking him into the arms of two MPs who had rushed over to investigate. Several other GIs confirmed what had happened, and without further ado the MPs took the Mexican away. And so it was that I arrived home two days later with bruised ribs, feeling secretly quite proud of myself.

The ten or so days spent at home on that third leave were somehow even less memorable than my previous furloughs. Unlike many, if not most, twenty-year-old GIs of that time, I had no girlfriend and had no idea of how or where to find one. It is certain that my mother fed me well, and I probably slept late every morning. I believe now that my stories of infantry life soon bored my family, even my two younger brothers, Stanley, age sixteen, and Donald, age ten.

Aside from the altercation with the knife-wielding Mexican-American in the depot at Columbus, the only episode I remember from that furlough happened one afternoon and evening on the return train trip from Chicago to Georgia. There were several college girls and GIs in the cars. Pints of whiskey were passed back and forth, and soon many of the tipsy girls had changed seats and were paired with a soldier.

I had a window seat, and one of the girls came to sit in the lap of a GI next to me, bringing a blanket with her. The GI and the girl insisted that I take a slug of whiskey from their pint, and I knew they hoped I would move to another seat to leave them alone. Not wanting to give up my window, I pretended to take a swallow, then turned away and feigned sleep. All that night I listened to the sound of heavy petting, felt the girl's warm hip bump against mine from time to time, but when dawn came she was back in her own seat. I never knew for sure how far the love-making under the blanket had managed to go.

On my return to Benning I learned that the division had once again been alerted to ship out on November 7, and all furloughs had been canceled on October 16, the day after I had left. But that move was also called off, and furloughs started up again. By December, Eisenhower's armies had virtually cleared France and the Lowlands and were closing in on the vaunted Siegfried Line and the Rhine River, while the Russians were nearing Germany from the east. It looked like our chances of seeing combat in Europe were slim; the war with Germany might be over by Christmas.

Up to this point our training had been limited to battalion-size exercises, but on December 12 the full division moved out to the field for joint maneuvers involving all three infantry regiments, plus artillery and attached combat-support units. During the remainder of December, with a brief respite for Christmas dinner back at Sand Hill, we must have walked a hundred miles, moved another hundred miles by truck, and dug foxholes in twenty different positions. And for the first time we experienced what it was like to attack, supported by dozens of tanks and scores of artillery pieces firing hundreds of live shells overhead, then lifting their fire just before we assaulted our assigned objective.

FIRING OUR MORTAR DURING FIELD EXERCISES

Meanwhile, on December 16, Hitler's desperate counterattack that has gone down in history as the Battle of the Bulge hit the U.S. First Army in the Ardennes, thus ending the widespread hopes that the war would end by Christmas. This sobering setback had its impact on the 71st Infantry Division.

On January 12 we received orders to move to the staging area at Camp Kilmer, New Jersey.

CHAPTER 6

CAMP KILMER AND THE USS *GENERAL TASKER BLISS*

January 12 to February 6, 1945

Camp Kilmer, New Jersey, was cold, and there was a foot of snow on the ground when we arrived. A week later, on about January 20, I was given a two-day pass and took the train up to Haddonfield, New Jersey, for an overnight stay with my Uncle Donald and Aunt Mildred Porter and their three kids, Jack, Craig, and Joyce. My sister, Kathleen, was there, too, as she had been in New York City on a visit involving her piano career, before returning to Colorado College in Colorado Springs to continue her graduate studies toward a masters degree in music. That one day and night in Haddonfield would be the last time I would see any of my family or relatives for nearly two years.

We left Camp Kilmer by troop train on January 25, 1945, and arrived at about midnight at a Staten Island pier. There, to the accompaniment of a small army band, we boarded a large U.S. Navy troop transport named the *General Tasker Bliss*. Red Cross girls passed out coffee and doughnuts, and each of us was given a ditty bag with a sewing kit, candy, and a paperback French-English dictionary and phrase book.

At the top of the gangway we were given a mess ticket and pointed toward the particular hold in which we would find our bunks. Each compartment housed about five hundred men, and was identified by a number and a phonetic letter, such as One Able, Two Baker, Three Charlie, and Four Dog. G Company found itself in compartment Four Dog, far down in the ship's bowels, close to the bilge.

At about 3:00 A.M. the ship's engines began to turn, but we were not allowed on deck until eight o'clock the next morning. By then we were well at sea, part of a large convoy, with no land in

MID ATLANTIC ON THE USS *GENERAL TASKER BLISS*

sight. As we stood by the rail on deck that first morning, gazing in awe at the gray Atlantic, we could see that the convoy included two or three dozen ships of all types and sizes, from large transports to small freighters and tankers. We were told reassuringly that our convoy was escorted by fifteen U.S. Navy destroyers and destroyer-escorts, but only a few of these could be seen on the horizon.

Our ship led the convoy with about five thousand men of the 5th Infantry Regiment and some division headquarters units on board, among them our new division commander, Maj. Gen. Willard G. Wyman, and the navy admiral in command of the convoy. Two other big transports, apparently identical to ours, carried the 14th and 66th Regiments and held station slightly aft of our port (left) and starboard (right) quarters. So the three big transports formed an arrowhead, with the rest of the convoy following behind in three columns. Convoy speed was probably about twelve knots—conforming to the slower speed of some of the tankers or freighters.

A rumor made the rounds that one of the smaller transports plowing along behind us carried nurses and Wacs. I remember that one GI jokingly threatened to jump overboard in the hope that he would be picked up by that smaller ship and make the rest of the trip in the company of females. But we never did learn if the rumor about the nurses and Wacs was true.

By the third day at sea we had memorized the many routine announcements that came over the loudspeaker, each beginning with "Now hear this, now hear this!" Then the order might be, "Sweepers, man your brooms! Clean sweepdown, fore and aft." Or each morning at dawn, when the smokers waited impatiently on deck, the welcome announcement would be, "The smoking lamp is lit." And at dusk the smokers would complain when they heard, "Now darken ship! The smoking lamp is out!" But as a nonsmoker, my favorite announcement came at mealtimes, when the speaker would say, "Now compartment Four Dog, form your chow line on the port side aft!"

Except for those who suffered from seasickness, chow time was a welcome break in the monotony, and I for one found the navy food exceptionally good. On the third day out, a few hundred miles northeast of Boston, we hit a severe storm, but I was one of a very few in our compartment who did not get sick as the big ship pitched and rolled. Proud of myself, I lorded it over the poor guys who missed chow and spent their time moaning in their bunks or rushing topside to lean over the rail. Taking advantage of the surplus food on the last day of that storm, I got in the chow line for seconds at lunch, and again at dinner. That was my mistake. The next day the sea was calm—almost like glass—but I suddenly became sick as a dog for a few hours, and took my share of razzing.

One GI from our platoon who razzed me was a machine gunner I liked, Eddie Charlon. After I got over my brief bout of *mal de mer*, he and I amused ourselves by playing game after game of chess with the small pocket set he carried.

There was a three-man jazz combo on board, consisting of two sax players and a trumpet, probably members of the division band. One night after dark this group came down to compartment Four Dog and, seated under the dim red light over the steel steps of the gangway, treated us to half an hour of jazz and sentimental *Hit Parade* tunes. For me, the best of these was a happy song I had not heard before, "The Sunny Side of the Street." The lyrics and tune have stayed with me all these years. It reminds me of a dark time when I was very afraid, way out in the mid-Atlantic ocean, said to be infested with U-boats.

Our crowded compartment, with bunks stacked five high and no places to sit except on the steel deck, soon began to smell like a locker room. We took saltwater showers every other day, forward in the shower room next to the head, as the navy calls its latrines. But these showers left us feeling sticky with salt and the residue of caustic GI soap lather.

I spent as much time as possible on deck, breathing the fresh salt air, watching the rise and fall of the ship's bows, or standing at her stern rail looking at her wake and at the ships behind us. I longed to be up on the bridge, and wondered how much privacy our officers had in their staterooms along the upper deck, known as "officers' country"—off-limits to enlisted men.

One day my assistant gunner, Glen Decker, and my two ammunition bearers and I were detailed to clean our head. This was a long, narrowing compartment in the very bow of the ship, on each side of which a dozen or so toilet seats were bolted to the sloping steel hull above long troughs through which a constant stream of seawater ran aft to a drain. My squad leader, Johnny Rohan, came in to inspect our job before admitting a line of waiting GIs, including another buck sergeant friend of his.

These two sergeants were always playing tricks on each other, and as we put away our pails and mops, Rohan whispered to me, "Watch this." With that he went to a seat nearest the forward bulkhead, a seat or two upstream from where his buddy sat, and dropped his pants. Then he wadded up a large ball of toilet paper, set it afire with his lighter, dropped it gently into the water trough, stood up quickly, pulled up his pants, and headed for the exit. We watched the burning wad float slowly along and pass under the bare bottom of Rohan's buddy. That sergeant jumped up like a jack-in-the-box, followed by several others sitting on the downstream seats.

"Goddamn you, Rohan, that's not funny!" his buddy shouted. "I'll getcha for that!"

Up on the forecastle of our ship, ahead of the bridge, was a circular steel platform on which was mounted a three-inch gun manned by a navy crew. Each afternoon at a set time the gun crew practiced removing the tarp, loading the gun, and training it out to port or starboard at an imaginary target. One afternoon, six or seven days into our voyage, they actually fired three or four live rounds at a target sled towed by a destroyer-escort out on the distant port flank. That started a rumor that we were approaching a known pack of waiting German U-boats.

That night, sometime after midnight, we heard the gong of the General Quarters alarm sound throughout the ship and an urgent voice on the loudspeaker said, "All hands man your battle stations!" This was followed by an order for all troops to put on their life jackets and prepare to move topside on order. A short minute later we heard a pounding of feet coming down into our compartment. We watched three sailors with flashlights move along the port side of the hull, looking for we knew not what.

They wouldn't tell us what had happened or what had caused the alarm, and soon after that, they left and went back up the stairway. Then the loudspeaker said, "All hands, secure from battle stations. Troops, remove your life jackets." The next morning, when I went topside, it appeared that half of the regiment was along the port rail, looking down. I joined them, and could see what looked like a long, slight dent in the ship's side, just above the waterline. Some said that a dud torpedo had hit us. Others said no, we had run into a piece of wreckage. The navy never did tell us what had caused the dent.

One sunny afternoon a sleek navy destroyer—probably a big new Sumner class with six five-inch guns in three dual mounts—appeared out of nowhere and came along our starboard side within megaphone hailing distance. The ensuing conversation seemed to be between the admiral on board our ship and the captain of the destroyer. Something was said about a new fleet of escorts coming out from England to meet our convoy that night, upon which this destroyer and some of our other escorts would head back west for home. The admiral replied, "Adiós, skipper. Good to have had you with us this far. Say hi to my son for me."

"Aye, aye, will do, Admiral," the destroyer captain replied. "Your son's doin' fine, by the way. Adiós and good luck."

Then, like a greyhound, the little warship surged forward in an impressive burst of speed, her wake boiling white. Within no more than fifteen minutes all we could see of her was her stick mast on the horizon ahead.

On our tenth day at sea we spotted a few seagulls, and the low coast of southwestern England appeared on the northeastern horizon. That afternoon we heard the voice of Major General Wyman on the loudspeaker: "Men, I am told the danger of German U-boats is behind us, and we'll arrive in Portsmouth Harbor tonight. Let's give the navy three big cheers for a safe journey!"

We cheered enthusiastically, and a short time later Wyman appeared among us on the main deck. He shook a few hands and asked how we were doing.

"Doin' just great, sir," several of us answered. That was the first time I had been close to our handsome division commander. The second time would be more than two months later, when he "hit the dirt" right behind me in a pile of manure as a few German artillery shells landed near the barn we were attacking.

Just before dusk that day, as we passed through the antisubmarine net protecting Portsmouth Harbor, the loudspeakers broadcast a BBC news program. The newscaster described the progress being made by British, Canadian, and American armies headed for the Rhine River as they mopped up the German remnants of the Battle of the Bulge. And he optimistically predicted that the Russians might reach Berlin in a week or two.

We listened to this news with mixed feelings. On the one hand, it might be nice to tell our children and grandchildren—if we survived to have any—that we had been in combat during the final kill of Hitler's Nazi Germany. On the other hand, I'm sure that many of us, like me, were secretly relieved to think that we might now survive the war for sure, and would serve only as occupation troops.

Our first and only view of England was of the waterfront docks and row houses of Portsmouth. We strained to see if there was any visible bomb damage. Then our attention was drawn to a small boat approaching us. Soon we could see that there were three uniformed figures standing on her foredeck, two of them wearing skirts! A young woman's British-accented voice came across the water by megaphone, asking, "What ship is that?"

A thousand lusty Yank voices shouted back, "The *General Tasker Bliss!*"

With that, the little boat came alongside, a ladder was swung out and lowered, and the three uniformed figures climbed aboard and saluted the navy ensign at the top. You can imagine the cacophony of whistles and admiring comments about the pretty legs as the two women—the equivalent of our navy's Waves—followed a braided English naval officer up another set of ladders to the bridge.

We dropped anchor shortly thereafter, and via the grapevine we learned that, although the plan had been for our three large troopships to cross the English Channel and dock at the French port of Le Havre that night, heavy fog made the crossing too risky and we would cross the next day.

Late afternoon on February 6, 1945, the *General Tasker Bliss* slowly threaded her way through the debris and wreckage of half-sunk cargo ships in the smashed harbor of Le Havre. Her GI passengers were permitted to come up topside for a last smoke before dark, and a first look at France. We crowded the rails, gaping at the destruction of war.

CHAPTER 7

LE HAVRE, CAMP OLD GOLD, AND THE ANCIENT SMELL OF FRANCE

February 6 to March 6, 1945

I remember the sad cry of the seagulls circling overhead, the tolling bells of the Channel marker buoys we passed, and the greenish color of the overcast French sky. Everything seemed to be tinted a sickly green hue that cast a pall over the rusting hulks of dead ships and the smashed warehouses and docks of Le Havre. I thought, *This is the color of death*. I sniffed the air for poisonous odors that might go with it, but the cold winter wind brought only the smell of seaweed and saltwater.

Forty miles down the coast lay the D-day beaches of Normandy, where thousands of Americans had died the previous June. Now, eight months later, contrary to the stories that Germany would be done for by the time we latecomers arrived, we knew that the war might last a while longer. We eased past several greenish masonry piers where a dock had once stood. On each pier was painted a black, evil-looking German skull-and-bones sign with crude letters proclaiming, *"Achtung! Minen!"*

"Look," I said to the guy next to me. "German for mines!"

"Ah," someone said, "they've cleared the mines by now."

"Then why'd they leave them old signs?" someone asked.

"So the brass kin take pictures. Look at 'em up there on the bridge."

We looked up at the bridge and saw several officers and two of our war correspondents focusing their cameras on the evil signs. As the ship nosed in to a long quay, we felt the engines rumble into reverse. Gangs of dungaree-clad men waited by the bollards. The sailors at the bow and stern of the *General Tasker Bliss* heaved lines down to the quay. Before the first gangplank was lowered, the ship's loudspeaker bellowed out the order "Now all army troops, lay below to your compartments!"

And so ended our first view of Le Havre. When we were permitted to come topside again it was quite dark, the harbor was foggy, rain was falling, and the city was completely blacked out.

The 5th Infantry Regiment finally set foot on French soil an hour before midnight on Sunday, February 6, 1945. G Company followed E and F Companies down the gangplank in the rain. We staggered under our loads of full field packs, weapons, and duffel bags. Sweating in our heavy overcoats, we cursed at the stupidity of the officers who had refused to let us put on raincoats and strap our overcoats onto our packs. An officer at the foot of the gangplank checked off each platoon and pointed down the quay to where our 2d Battalion executive officer, Maj. Irving Heymont, stood.

"C'mon, move it along there, move it along!" Heymont kept shouting.

"Ah, shove it up yer ass," an exasperated and anonymous voice said from somewhere, and we all snickered. But under Heymont's tirade, our tall and broad-beamed company commander, Captain Neal, formed us in a column of twos behind F Company, and we double-timed down the long quay and across a muddy field. Neal led us to where a line of odd-looking army semitrailer cattle trucks—normally used to transport supplies and ammunition—waited in the dark. By that time the 2d Battalion's other companies were already loaded aboard their trucks and the convoy was ready to roll.

Unlike the standard six-by-six trucks we were used to, the trailers in which we rode were topless, with removable wooden stake sides. They had no benches, so we sat on our packs and duffel bags. About forty miserable infantrymen were packed like sardines in each vehicle. The rain diminished to a drizzle as our convoy, with dimmed blackout lights, made its way slowly through the wet streets of Le Havre and out onto a deserted highway, where the land smelled strange and musty.

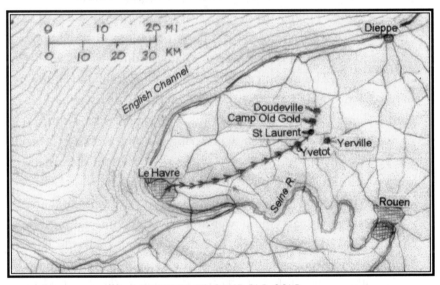

LE HAVRE TO CAMP OLD GOLD

We grew cold and were thankful now for our overcoats with the broad collars turned up around our ears. The cold began to have its usual effect on our bladders, as we had been given no chance to relieve ourselves before loading up. Sometime in the wee hours of the morning the convoy crossed a railroad and stopped in a town we identified as Yvetot, from the sign on its patched-up railroad station.

"Thank gawd!" someone said. "Piss call at last. Jeez, my teeth are floating. How d'ya pernounce the name o' this here burg, anyway? *Yevvey-tote* or what? What kinda name is that?"

"It's pronounced *Veto,* ya dummy," said another GI, who claimed to speak French.

"Well," said the first GI, "I'm gonna take me a pee in *Vee-tow!*" and started to climb over the tailgate.

"Stay on the damn truck!" said a sergeant. "We're movin' out agin. Ya kin just hold it like the rest of us!"

Our halfhearted laughter was lost in the sound of grinding gears as the trucks started moving again. Soon we were all complaining. The men in the other trucks joined us in chanting *"Piss call! Piss call!"* Finally the convoy stopped on the outskirts of a small farm village. Amid the clanging of tailgates we climbed down and stood in the dark along a roadside ditch to relieve our full bladders. The moon came from behind a cloud and illuminated a stucco farmhouse with blue shutters on its windows, across the ditch from where I stood. I thought I saw a shutter move slightly, and I shivered, wondering uncomfortably if some old French farmer and his wife, whose sleep we had disturbed, were watching as we stood there with our flies unbuttoned.

Everything looked strange and foreign to me. Even the shape of the steel poles carrying power and telephone lines alongside the road looked alien. The nearby fields and apple orchards, barren in the cold moonlight, gave off the same pungent odor we had smelled earlier. I thought *This is the ancient smell of French soil, soaked in the blood of hundreds of wars, worn out by thousands of harvests, graveyard to untold generations of Gauls and Romans and God knows who came before them.*

The U.S. Army had named its staging areas in France after popular—or not so popular—cigarette brands. It was rumored that the best of these was Camp Lucky Strike, fittingly named for one of the more popular brands. That camp was said to have good food, hot showers, pretty Red Cross girls, a PX with beer, and a nightly USO show with Hollywood starlets. Naturally, we hoped that Lucky Strike was to be our destination, but no such luck, and we never did learn if the stories about it were true.

Just after sunrise our long regimental convoy passed through a small town called St. Laurent, topped a rise, and a few hundred yards short of another small town called Doudeville, we halted in front of a huge tent city in a muddy field. A sign proclaimed this to be Camp Old Gold—fittingly named after what our smokers said was by far the worst-tasting cigarette brand of all.

It was a cold, hungry, and disappointed bunch of infantrymen who lined up for the roll call as the empty cattle trucks turned around and headed back up the road. Our officers went off to a meeting with the battalion commander, our mess sergeant and his cooks were sent down to a pyramid tent that was to serve as the battalion kitchen, and the rest of us waited. We stamped our boots in the frozen mud and watched the cooks unload gasoline stoves, water cans, and boxes of rations from the kitchen trucks that had brought up the rear of our convoy.

When our officers returned we gathered around our pimply-faced platoon leader, 2d Lt. Joseph A. Tyler, who read off the weapons platoon tent assignments. He assigned his platoon runner, platoon medic, and the 2d and 3d Mortar Squads to a twelve-man tent with a duckboard floor, folding canvas cots, and a small cast-iron stove with a rickety stovepipe that rose through an opening in the tent roof. The two squad leaders democratically had the lowly buck privates draw straws to decide who would get the two coveted cots nearest the stove. But whoever the winners were, they were sorry when it began to rain and the water leaked onto their cots from the hole in the tent roof.

We stowed our gear, donned our raincoats, and went to find the company latrine. This was a long, narrow slit trench up the hill behind the tents, with planks placed crosswise so a man could squat with his boots on the plank instead of in the mud.

One of the gullible GIs who had swallowed the story about Camp Lucky Strike was a tall, gangly Irish kid in the 2d Squad named Luther Hayes, from Boston. Because he had been so sure we were going to the fabulous Lucky Strike, we began to call him Lucky. As we made our first visit to the latrine we kidded him unmercifully.

"Jeez, Lucky," we said, "after we take a crap let's go down to the mess tent and see if they're gonna serve us T-bone steaks for chow. And maybe we can get some coffee and doughnuts from those gorgeous Red Cross girls. Boy, Lucky, I bet ya can hardly wait to see them Hollywood starlets at the USO show tonight!"

Before noon chow we went down to the supply tent to pick up our duffel bags, extra blankets, and our ration of coal for the stove. Each tent received one bucket of coal per day, but we soon learned that this lasted only about two hours if we weren't careful. That night Rohan and Bailey enlisted me and one or two others to raid the officers' ample coal pile. We made raids on that pile almost every night until we left Camp Old Gold. It was lucky we weren't caught.

Although it was midwinter, we found it remarkable that there was no snow whatsoever during the weeks we were at Camp Old Gold, nor do I recall much rain. But the temperature fell below freezing every night, and no matter how many layers of clothes we wore at night under our extra blankets, we were always cold. We were allowed to use candles with the tent flaps shut, but the candles were in short supply. In addition to Rohan's nightly coal-stealing forays, we were impressed with his ingenuity when he came back from the mess tent with cans of solidified grease and some heavy string. These he somehow fashioned into crude wick-type lamps; they were smelly but better than no light at all.

The hot meals served by our battalion kitchen were just so-so, and the servings were not large, so we were always very hungry. Although we were warned not to eat the local vegetables because the French farmers fertilized their fields with "night soil"—human excrement—it didn't much matter. I don't recall seeing so much as one Brussels sprout, potato, rutabaga, or any other winter vegetable in any of the barren fields thereabouts. And if the locals had any such things in their cellars, they didn't offer them for sale. But they did offer us eggs and bread in exchange for cigarettes. Using my French phrase book, I soon learned to say "*Je voudrai acheter des oeufs*" (I would like to buy some eggs) or "*du pain*" (some bread).

The camp was off-limits to the French, and we saw few of them on the road. One night at dusk after retreat, Waitus Hatley, Roland Vincent, and I took a walk toward the little town of Doudeville and were approached by a teenage French boy who asked, "*Cigarette pour mon Papa?*"

We gave him a pack of cigarettes. His name was Claude, and he lived on a nearby farm. We asked if he would sell us some eggs in exchange for more cigarettes, and arranged to meet him the next evening at the same time and place. At that second meeting we exchanged two packs of cigarettes for a dozen eggs, and even threw in a candy bar for good measure. Boy, how that kid's face lit up! The next time we met he invited the three of us to dinner the following Sunday afternoon, and we readily accepted.

Thus we got to know the Jouen family. We showed up loaded with cigarettes, a few cigars, candy, K rations, two cans of Spam, and a can of coffee someone had stolen from the mess tent. In exchange, the Jouens served us the best they had. I remember some kind of chicken and barley soup, an omelette, and thick slices of sour bread. We were amused as Claude's father, who sat at the head of the table, held the huge loaf of bread in one arm, cut the slices with a large knife, and good-naturedly tossed them, one by one, down the long, bare plank table to his three American guests, and then to his nine kids and his wife. This was done as a kind of game.

MEMORABLE SUNDAY DINNER WITH THE JOVEN FAMILY

At the end of the meal Claude was sent down to the cellar, and soon he returned with two bottles. His father closed one eye, took aim at a large earthenware bowl his mother had set in the middle of the table, then with a flourish popped the cork on the first bottle and a foamy white stream of what turned out to be hard cider shot up in an arc, directly into the bowl. He repeated the performance with the second bottle, and we all clapped.

I remember thinking how my parents would disapprove, but I told myself it would be impolite to refuse as I gingerly drank a cup of the burning stuff, trying not to cough. I will always remember that dinner with the only French family I got to know during our stay at Camp Old Gold. We were touched when Claude's parents asked us to call them "Papa" and "Mama."

None of them spoke English, and we spoke only a little French, but we all managed to communicate with much waving of hands and looking up of words in our French-English dictionaries.

On February 27, 1945, two days after that meal with the Jouen family, I wrote home about it, but of course I did not mention the hard cider. I wrote that Claude worked with his father in a local silo, and recorded his and his brothers' and sisters' names and ages. For the record, they were Claude, age sixteen; Jacqueline, fifteen; Roland, thirteen; Simone, eleven; Lucien, nine; Mauriciette, seven; Denise, five; Pierette, four; and Jean-Pierre, three.

Perhaps it is wishful thinking, but I seem to recall that the oldest girl, Jacqueline, was very pretty. We three Americans tried hard to strike up a conversation with her, but without much success, as she was quite shy. But she did write down the names and ages of her siblings for me. Today, if still living, she would be about seventy-two years old.

Our outgoing letters had been censored since Camp Kilmer, so I could only write home that we were in France. I wrote home at least twice a week, and each letter included a request for cookies or anything sweet. This was necessary because each package sent from the States required a specific request, and the post office "canceled" each request with a rubber stamp before accepting the package.

Letters from home took from two to three weeks to reach us, and packages took even longer. In one letter my father mentioned that a business acquaintance of his—now an army captain with the Corps of Engineers in Denver—claimed that after I had been in a place for two weeks, censorship rules allowed me to give its name. Acting on this misinformation, I wrote that we had landed at Le Havre and were stationed at Camp Old Gold near the town of St. Laurent. That letter was returned to me unapproved by Lieutenant Tyler, who censored all of our platoon's outgoing mail. My irritation at that Stateside captain showed in a later letter in which I said, in effect, that he was all wet.

From then on I was more careful, but I tried to give as much local color as possible. In one letter I told of a proud old Frenchman in his Sunday best, riding the largest horse I had ever seen—maybe a French Percheron. The horse was in his Sunday best, too, decked out in a fancy harness and saddle. In another letter I included a sketch of a French farmhouse. After receiving our first pay in francs, I wrote that we were now receiving a 20 percent increase for overseas duty, and I sent home a number of colorful French franc notes, worth about a dollar at the exchange rate of two cents per franc.

There was not much to do with our leisure time except write letters, play volleyball or touch football in the mud, and walk down the road to visit Doudeville after evening chow. A typical day began with an hour of calisthenics, followed by duties such as filling in old latrines and digging new ones. The hour before retreat at dusk was always spent cleaning weapons. Once or twice a Red Cross Clubmobile came around and passed out coffee and doughnuts, but I recall the Red Cross girls as being old and ugly, the doughnuts as stale, and the coffee as worse than that served at our battalion mess.

One Sunday afternoon we were treated to a division band concert and a third-rate USO show. The concert was okay, but the show was a flop; not a single name actor or actress appeared on the crude stage.

Until the last week of our stay at Camp Old Gold there were no showers and not enough coal to heat water on our tent stove, so we used our steel helmets to shave and take cold-water sponge baths. God, were we dirty! Finally, as the end of February approached, we were told that Ike Eisenhower himself was coming to inspect the 71st Infantry Division. With that news, our engineer battalion rigged up some cold-water showers in which we were at least able to get rid of some of the grime and wash our clothes.

The charismatic Ike—by then wearing the five stars of a general of the army—inspected the 5th Infantry Regiment on about

March 1, and I for one was thrilled as he walked past our ranks, followed by Major General Wyman and Colonel Wooten. Some said the purpose of Eisenhower's visit was to determine if the 71st was ready for combat. This came as somewhat of a surprise, as the GI newspaper *Stars and Stripes* had for several days been reporting a general offensive all along the front that might end the war in a week. This news had convinced many of us that we would never see combat but would be sent into Germany as occupation troops after it was all over.

Perhaps we should have guessed how wrong we were when, the night after Eisenhower's inspection, we made the first of two night marches in full field gear to practice cross-country night patrols, and a few days later were sent out to a nearby rifle range to fire our weapons. Sergeant Rohan, as squad leader, was armed with the only M1 rifle in our squad. My assistant gunner, Glen Decker, and I carried .45-caliber automatic pistols, and our two ammunition bearers, Hatley and Vincent, were armed with the new light carbine, which was not very effective beyond one hundred or two hundred yards. But we all had a turn at firing the M1 rifle again. It was accurate to five hundred yards. There would come a day, a few weeks later, when I wished I had an M1, as my .45 pistol was useless at ranges beyond fifty feet. But another day came when I took over as squad leader, and after that I gladly carried the M1 through my last forty-four days in combat.

The march to the rifle range took us north through Doudeville and almost to the coastal city of Dieppe. On the return march we passed a large farmyard in which several barefoot men, women, and children were stomping red grapes in a large circular vat. Laughing and waving, they gestured to us to come join them in their fun. I am sure several of the wine drinkers among us would have done so gladly in exchange for a bottle of wine, but we marched on down the road to Doudeville and back to our tent city.

The next morning it was official: We were going up to the front the following day! That night I joined several others on a walk to the larger town of St. Laurent. We found a large bistro with a sawdust floor and smelling of spilled beer. An old French farmer offered us a bottle of Calvados, but after one sip of the fiery apple brandy I vowed once again to remain a teetotaler. With one exception, I kept that vow until the war ended.

On Tuesday morning, March 6, 1945, we were told to remove our division shoulder patches, and several trucks pulled up with boxes of live ammunition. We filed by the open crates as our supply sergeant passed out clips, extra bandoliers of ammunition, and two hand grenades per man. If I had any lingering doubts about our destination up to that point, they were dispelled by those two pineapple-shaped hand grenades, which I put in one of the large side pockets of my field jacket.

Part II

Combat Infantryman

MARCH 6 TO MAY 8, 1945

CHAPTER 8

TO THE FRONT BY RAIL, TRUCK, AND JEEP

March 6 to 11, 1945

It was a somber bunch of 71st Division infantrymen who loaded on dozens of six-by-six trucks the afternoon of March 6 for the short ride to the railhead at Yerville, a few miles south of St. Laurent. As I thought back over all that had gone wrong with my plans since volunteering for induction twenty months earlier, it was a bitter pill to swallow. I thought of all the letters in which I had written the prophecy that the war would end before we saw any combat. I thought *Dean, what a stupid optimist you have been!*

But no longer! Now I was fast becoming more of a pessimistic fatalist, and although I was already somewhat of an agnostic, I decided it wouldn't hurt to say a prayer when I sensed the cold shadow of death coming ever nearer.

War history buffs may remember stories of the doughboys sent to France during World War I in 1917 and 1918, and how they rode up to the front in tiny forty-by-eight boxcars. These were so named by the French because their capacity was *quarante hommes* or *huit chevaux*—forty men or eight horses. I was something of a war history buff, so I felt as if the clock had been set back a quarter century when I saw what looked like the same old forty-by-eights making up our troop train at Yerville.

Each car had a few bales of straw that were broken open to serve as bedding, but loaded down as we were with our weapons, combat packs, and one duffel bag per man, there was no way forty of us could have been squeezed into one of those little rattletraps. Even the thirty-odd men of G Company's weapons platoon were tightly cramped in the boxcar to which we were assigned.

G-COMPANY LOADING ON FORTY BY EIGHTS

With a shrill *peep-peep* of the locomotive's whistle and a banging of couplings, our train left the Yerville yards some time after noon and headed east, toward the front. We seldom traveled at speeds of more than twenty-five miles per hour and made frequent short stops for piss call. Three scheduled stops per day—morning, noon, and late afternoon—were long enough for us to get off and build fires alongside the tracks to heat up our C rations and water for coffee. Our route took us north of Paris, then east to Nancy and Luneville. After two days and nights we detrained at Lenning in the Vosges Mountain foothills of the province of Alsace-Lorraine.

I was so depressed and withdrawn during most of that train ride across northern France that I have very little memory of the passing countryside, or of towns made famous during World War I.

I can recall only a few incidents worth telling: The first involved a loudmouthed tough guy whose last name, I think, was Wilson. During one of our stops Glen Decker and I decided to break the monotony by riding up in the little cupola atop the caboose at the rear of our train. For some reason there were no French trainmen riding up there. I suppose if the train had any brakemen they were asleep in the caboose itself. Well, loudmouth Wilson—a gunner in one of our platoon's two machine-gun squads—decided to join us up in our lofty perch.

When he realized we were not impressed with his blustering tirades about how he hated the Krauts and would be fearless in combat, he suddenly shouted, "By God, I'll show you!" and smashed out a pane of glass with his bare fist, cutting himself badly. Needless to say, after we returned to our boxcar at the next stop we steered clear of that nut. But there would be a later incident, in actual combat, when he once again stupidly made a tough-guy scene.

A second incident during that train ride brought home the fact that the war was getting close. As we neared the city of

Nancy, a dozen sleek Douglas A-20 light attack bombers flew over, headed east toward the front. Half an hour later we counted only eleven of them in the returning formation. A few minutes after that we heard the unmistakable sound of sputtering engines and saw the last of the A-20s coming back very low, one engine out with its propeller feathered, and the other engine trailing smoke—just like in the newsreels.

In midafternoon came the third memorable incident. We pulled into the rail yards at Nancy and stopped beneath a pedestrian overpass. On this walkway stood dozens of waving French people, many of them girls in colorful skirts. Among the girls were several khaki-clad GIs we took to be rear-area support troops. Then we heard several harmonicas and an accordion playing, and saw that some of the GIs and girls were dancing. That was the one cheerful sight I remember from our trip to the front. How we wished we could get off and join those lucky rear-echelon bastards up on that overpass! But it was not to be. After taking on coal and water, our locomotive's whistle emitted its *peep-peep,* and we were on our way again.

Just before dusk, after passing through Luneville, we unloaded at the small town of Lenning, and from there the 2d Battalion, 5th Infantry, was taken by truck to a smaller village in Alsace, where we arrived after dark. The village was not far from the town of Sarrebourg. To the tune of distant artillery rumbling a few miles to the east, G Company formed ranks in a narrow street, and each platoon was assigned to a house or a hayloft for the night. The five squads of our weapons platoon—two machine-gun squads and three mortar squads—were assigned to a second-story hayloft over one of the old houses. Access to the loft was by an exterior ladder, so each squad formed a chain to pass up our packs and heavy duffel bags.

The hay in the loft was warm and dry, and we were warned not to smoke up there for fear of fire. We were also warned not to fraternize with any civilians we might see in this village, because

HAYLOFT BILLETS AT AN ALSATIAN VILLAGE

it was said that some of them might be German spies. It had been only a week or two since the Germans had left and retreated toward the Rhine River. The Germanic names of the towns in the region attested to the fact that Alsace had once been part of Germany and had changed hands many times as a result of many wars. We were told that most of the people spoke German, and many were thought to be Nazi sympathizers if not outright spies. I for one didn't see a civilian during our short stay in that village.

At this point it seems appropriate to summarize what the overall situation was on the Western Front in Europe by that second week in March 1945.

The six Allied armies under Eisenhower's SHAEF command in northwestern Europe were stretched over a front of nearly four hundred miles, from Holland in the north to Switzerland to the south. More than three hundred miles of that front was manned by a million or more American combat troops supported by another million or two in the rear areas, including the Eighth and Ninth U.S. Army Air Forces. This compares with perhaps three hundred thousand British and Canadian combat troops along a fifty-mile front on the far northern flank, and no more than one hundred thousand French combat troops—all equipped with American arms—along a shorter front on the far southern flank.

The British Second and Canadian First Armies under Field Marshal Bernard Montgomery were ever so slowly battering their way through Holland toward the lower Rhine. On Monty's right flank the U.S. Ninth Army under General William Simpson had entered a corner of Germany and would soon reach the west bank of the Rhine opposite Dusseldorf.

South of the Ninth was General Omar Bradley's Twelfth Army Group, composed of General Courtney Hodges' U.S. First Army and General George Patton's Third Army. These two armies had mopped up after the Battle of the Bulge, cleared the Germans out of Belgium and Luxembourg, and were both now on German soil. Part of the Third Army was nearing Koblenz, and part was preparing to attack through the Saar region toward the Rhine cities of Mainz and Worms.

To complete the picture, the Sixth Army Group under General Jacob Devers, made up of General Alexander Patch's U.S. Seventh Army and General Jean de Lattre de Tassigny's French First Army, were holding primarily defensive positions on the southern part of the front. The Seventh Army was in the Vosges Mountains, facing a segment of the Siegfried Line that extended west from the Rhine to Saarbrücken, and the French First Army was deployed along the Rhine from Strasbourg to the Swiss border at Basel.

Of course, we enlisted men of the 71st Infantry Division had only a general idea of this overall situation, pieced together from stories and maps in *Stars and Stripes*. We were told only that we were now in the Seventh Army. For security reasons, it would be weeks before news of our arrival at the front was released.

On Saturday afternoon, March 10, 1945, we received orders to turn in our duffel bags to G Company's supply sergeant and make ready for the last leg of our trip to the front. We were told that trucks would arrive before dark to take us from our little village up to a "quiet" sector in which the green 71st Infantry Division would relieve the veteran 100th Infantry Division on a ridge in the Vosges, a few miles to the east.

It was still daylight when we heard the distant grind of approaching trucks, and our nervous platoon leader, Lt. Joseph Tyler, prematurely ordered us down from our hayloft to form up in the street. The convoy passed by without stopping, and an angry Captain Neal gave poor Tyler a royal chewing-out. We silently cursed Tyler as we wearily climbed back up the ladder to the loft. There we waited and waited. It was well after dark when the trucks on which we were to ride to the front finally arrived.

What a miserable ride it was. Within a mile or two we turned off the road, and from that point the convoy traveled cross-country, much of the time winding its way slowly through dense evergreen forests, trying to avoid the ditches alongside the trail.

Our drivers were exhausted, having already made an earlier trip up to the front. As a result, many trucks ended up in a ditch that night. Traveling with blackout lights, it was hard for them to see the ditches and keep contact with the truck ahead unless they maintained close intervals, and this resulted in many sudden stops and grinding starts. Our driver lost sight of the truck ahead several times, and in desperation he turned on his headlights as he accelerated to catch up. This scared the hell out of us. We were sure German observers on the high mountain ahead would call in a salvo of artillery. But all we heard was our own big guns firing from somewhere up ahead.

Lieutenant Tyler rode next to the driver in the cab of our truck, which was fitted with a large steel ring on which a .30-caliber machine gun was mounted. From time to time he stood up with his head above the ring to help guide our driver through the trees. He was standing thus when the truck ahead stopped suddenly. Our driver swerved, and the gun ring struck the trunk of a passing tree. Poor Tyler hit his helmeted head hard against the ring and was knocked cold. He came to quickly, but had it not been for his helmet he would have been seriously hurt. Our platoon sergeant, Al Feltman, helped him into the back of the truck and made him lie down, then took his place in the cab.

As we emerged from the woods at last, we saw the glow of artificial moonlight created by searchlights bouncing their beams off of the low-hanging clouds, and we could see flares bursting over a high ridge to the east. We were getting closer to our destination.

As usual, the jarring truck ride had its effect on our bladders, and several of us began to complain. Our two section leaders, Staff Sergeants Cree and Rodewald, told us to go ahead and piss in our helmets if we couldn't hold it, then pass the helmets back from man to man to those sitting nearest the tailgate, who would throw the contents overboard. My seat on the bench was just behind the cab, so I was spared the job of passing helmets other than my own. You should have heard the others on the benches swear whenever a helmet was passed and the truck hit a bump! I suspect that they spilled more warm piss on themselves and the packs at their feet than ever made it over the tailgate.

We finally came out onto a paved road at about 11:00 P.M., and soon we pulled into a large square paved with brick in the center courtyard of some sort of bombed-out factory complex. We saw bright flashes on a nearby ridge atop a sheer cliff across the square, and heard the unmistakable coughing of a battery of 4.2-inch heavy mortars lobbing shells overhead toward the enemy lines. Now and then we could make out the tiny silhouettes of gunners rising to drop projectiles into the tubes while other soldiers ran forward with more ammunition. I imagined a scene from Dante's *Inferno*, with geysers of molten lava illuminating frenzied dancers cavorting around their fires.

Each flash from those mortars was reflected in the water of a circular fountain in the center of the rubble-strewn square. In the light we could see that the glass from all of the narrow windows in the pockmarked stone wall of the old factory had been blown out.

We dismounted near the large, doorless entrance to one of the largest factory buildings, and after the still-dazed Lieutenant Tyler had been helped down, Sergeant Feltman formed us in ranks of squads to count heads. Then he and Tyler and the two section leaders—Cree and Rodewald—went off to report to Captain Neal, who stood by the fountain with the other company officers and senior NCOs.

Soon the battalion commander's jeep drove up. We strained to hear what the officers were saying, but the nearly continuous slamming of the mortars up on the ridge drowned out their voices.

After the jeep left, Cree came back and gathered his three mortar squads in a circle. He said the Germans had been sporadically shelling the square, warned us not to smoke or show any lights, then told us to bed down under cover just inside the open doorway behind us. He said the bombed-out complex had been a glass factory, and he warned us not to explore the upper floors, as only the ground floor had been cleared of booby traps.

Decker, Hatley, Vincent, and I followed Johnny Rohan into the dark factory, cautiously feeling our way along the concrete floor to the right, kicking aside pieces of rubble and glass. In the flashes of light coming through the high windows, Rohan found a clear area where he had us drop our packs. The floor felt sticky, and I grumbled that we should search for a cleaner place, but Rohan wouldn't listen, and I was so dog-tired I didn't argue. I spread my shelter half and blankets on the grimy concrete and, using my pack for a pillow, slept fitfully for the few hours remaining until dawn.

CHAPTER 9

THE FRONT AT SKYLINE DRIVE

Sunday, March 11, 1945

The noise of a truck pulling up outside the glass factory woke me at dawn on what was to be my first full day of front-line combat. I looked up to see dirty cobwebs hanging from shelf after shelf of dusty glass vases and tumblers that reflected the gray light coming through the narrow windows. Rohan had already gone outside, leaving his neatly rolled pack behind. There was a dry taste of grit in my mouth, and when I saw that my hands and pack were black with grime from the oily concrete floor, I cursed loudly, waking my elfish little assistant gunner, Glen Decker.

"That goddamn Rohan!" I swore, seeing the black smears on Decker's face. "Just *look* at this black shit! I *told* him this wasn't a good place to sack out, but he wouldn't listen."

My tirade woke up our two ammunition bearers, Hatley and Vincent, and they laughed when they saw Decker's and my dirty faces and hands. They had luckily bedded down in a relatively clean spot. Decker and I rummaged through our packs for bars of soap and green GI towels, shed our overcoats and field jackets, put on our helmets, buckled on our pistol belts, and went outside to look for a place to wash. We joined a few other GIs around the fountain, stripped off our woolen OD shirts and winter undershirts, and used our helmets to dip water from the shallow pool. The water was cold and dirty, but it was better than nothing, and we managed to remove the worst of the grime from our hands and faces.

G Company's two jeeps and the kitchen truck were parked close to the foot of the cliff across the square. A line of sleepy GIs were filling their canteens from a tripod-mounted water bag as they shuffled up to the open bed of the truck from which one of our cooks was dispensing hot coffee from the spigot of a large urn. Decker and I hurriedly put on our shirts, pulled our aluminum canteens and cups from the canvas pouches hooked to our pistol belts, and ran to join the line across the square.

We saw Rohan and our other two mortar squad leaders by one of the jeeps, coffee cups in hand, looking at a map with Sergeant Feltman, Lieutenant Tyler, and Captain Neal. We were close enough to hear Neal say, "Okay then, odd man wins," and the three squad leaders each flipped a coin. We wondered what kind of game they were playing.

When the cook had filled our cups with black coffee he told us that Captain Neal had ordered the kitchen to serve a last hot breakfast before we went up on the line. Although my stomach had tightened into a knot from imagining what lay ahead, I tried to be funny and said something like, "Make mine a steak, very rare, and my eggs sunny side up, please."

"Listen, Mac," the cook said, "yer gonna git Spam and powdered eggs! Take it 'er leave it."

The sun was up by the time Decker, Hatley, Vincent, and I sat down with our backs against the stone wall of the factory to eat what was to be our last hot breakfast for several weeks.

Between mouthfuls of greasy Spam and tasteless powdered eggs, the four of us talked in subdued voices, remarking on the fact that the 4.2-inch mortars on the ridge above the cliff had ceased firing sometime before dawn. Although the front was said to be no more than a mile or two to the northeast, we could hear no sound of artillery or small-arms fire. The silence seemed to confirm that the green 71st was to take over a quiet sector.

HOT BREAKFAST AT A GLASS FACTORY

I thought, *Dear God, how happy I would be if the Krauts decided to surrender right now, before I see so much as one battlefield.* As I was musing thus, Rohan joined us with a full mess kit, and I could see that he was excited about something. Still angry about the dirt and grime I had accumulated from the grease-smeared factory floor, I answered his cheerful greeting with a mumbled grunt.

But it was hard to stay mad at Johnny Rohan for long. Although he wore three stripes and I wore but one, he never pulled rank and usually treated me as his equal. As we walked over to wash our mess kits in the drums of scalding hot water by the kitchen truck, he whispered that he had some good news, and I brightened up a bit.

"You and me are lucky," he said. "We don't have to hike up to the line like the rest of the company. We're gonna *ride* up!"

"How come?" I asked.

"The Old Man wants us to take a mortar and a radio up this morning to get a look at the layout in daylight," he explained. "Just the two of us. The 100th Division is gonna send a jeep down to pick us up at about ten o'clock. Better get your stuff ready."

"This *morning*?" I croaked. "In broad *daylight*?" I felt myself getting angry again.

"Yeah. The Old Man wants us up there early, so the guys we're relieving can show us where to lay down some fire in case the Krauts are wise to the fact that the 100th is being relieved after dark tonight by green troops, and they decide to pull off an attack."

"What about the other mortar squads?" I asked. "How come the captain picked us?"

"He didn't. We flipped coins, odd man out, and I won."

"Oh, *great*! You call that winning?"

Rohan grinned and said, "Sure, why not? You wanna walk up carryin' a mortar? Jeez, Joy, I thought you'd jump at the chance to ride. Anyway, the cap'n is happy I won, and he knows you're the best gunner in the company. He told me we'll have the honor of being the first two guys from G Company to go up—maybe even the first from the whole division."

I wanted to tell John Rohan to take that honor and *shove* it! I tried not to show my fear as I walked back to get the rest of my gear from the factory, leaving him to explain the plan to Decker and the others. I thought, *My God, in just two hours I will be headed for the front line in a jeep!*

At about 9:00 A.M. the company was assembled in the court-yard for a welcome announcement. Our supply truck had arrived with a supply of the army's latest-style sleeping bags, and we were told to turn in our shelter halves and one of the two blankets we carried. Then our supply sergeant demonstrated how the sleeping bags worked. By today's standards they were a joke, but at the time we were happy to have them.

This new sleeping bag was made from blanket material, tapered and sewed together with a zipper. This sack was inserted into a waterproof tapered bag, also with a zipper. It would keep us warmer than two blankets and a shelter half. We wondered why the army's Quartermaster Corps hadn't come up with the idea much sooner.

After my dirty pack was rolled with the new sleeping bag in it and I had cleaned my Colt .45 pistol, there was nothing to do for half an hour while I waited for the jeep to come down from the front line to get us. I joined Decker and one or two others who decided to explore the first floor of the bombed-out glass factory. Much of the glassware on the shelves was cracked or broken, but I soon found six small, unbroken crystal goblets that matched, and decided to send them home the first chance I got. I wrapped them in a pair of socks and stuffed them into my field jacket pocket with my two hand grenades. I threw the goblets away two or three days later.

I was able to trade my grimy pack for a clean one a few weeks later. It was taken from a sad pile of gear that had belonged to men who were dead or wounded.

The 100th Division jeep arrived at about 10:00 A.M. and braked to a stop in the courtyard just as Captain Neal finished giving Rohan and me our final instructions, with Feltman listening. We loaded our packs and the 60mm mortar into the back of the jeep, and Neal and Feltman wished us luck. I rode in the backseat with the gear, and Rohan sat up front next to the driver, his M1 rifle across his lap and the walkie-talkie radio slung around his neck. Showing off, the driver accelerated out of the court-yard, and I had to hold on tight to avoid being thrown out.

As was the usual practice this close to the front, the jeep's windshield was folded down flat on the hood to minimize any re-flection that might be spotted by an observer. I felt the wind strong in my face when we came out onto the paved road doing what felt like sixty miles per hour. We sped up a straight section of road for half a mile. Off in an open field to the left I saw a bat-tery of four 105mm howitzers, their snouts protruding from be-neath camouflage nets. One of the shirtless cannoneers waved at us, and I waved back. The driver seemed to speed up even more then, and he turned to Rohan and said, "Ever now an' then the fuckin' Krauts throw a few 88s in here, tryin' t'git them guns. But this here stretch is the only bad part. Once we git to them woods up front, y'all kin relax until we git up to where yer goin'."

It was then that I noticed a few shell holes in the field close to the road, each ringed with burned grass. I felt my heart pound-ing until we reached the line of trees at the foot of the ridge. A square sign was nailed to one of the trees:

> CAUTION—MINES!
> ROAD CLEARED TO
> SHOULDERS ONLY!

Beyond this sign the road narrowed, and our driver slowed down to pass through the splintered remains of a log breast-work. He pointed at the empty foxholes behind the logs and said, "Kraut roadblock. We killed three of the bastards here a couple of weeks ago."

We drove deeper into the dark, spooky forest, following a telephone wire strung from limb to limb, and soon we came to a fork in the narrow dirt road where a sign with two arrows was nailed to a tree trunk. The sign was freshly painted in black let-ters and looked something like this:

←2D BN HQ   2 KM

SKYLINE DRIVE   1 KM→

"I painted that sign myself an' put it up this morning," the driver said proudly as he stopped the jeep to admire his work. "That's so yer guys won't git lost when they come up to relieve us after dark tonight."

I assumed we would be going to the 2d Battalion command post, so I was surprised when the driver shifted into low gear and turned right.

"The company yer gonna relieve is up here on Skyline Drive," he explained. "I'll drop ya off at the CP. It's in the only house that can't be seen from the Kraut positions."

And so it was that sometime before noon on Sunday, March 11, 1945, our jeep ground its way slowly up the steep switchback road to the top of the ridge and stopped in front of a stone house with attached barn. There was no one around; it was quiet as a graveyard. Not even a dog barked. Our driver called softly, "Hey! Anyone home?"

No one appeared, and he called again. Finally, from the cellar door of a house across the road, a grimy-looking GI with lather on his face came out. He looked like one of Bill Mauldin's famous cartoon GI characters.

"What can I do for ya, Mac?" he asked.

"These are the two mortar guys from the 5th Infantry," our driver explained. "Should I drop 'em off here?"

"Nah," the half-shaved GI replied. "Why doncha take 'em on up to the weapons platoon CP, third house on the left."

"Shit no, man!" the driver said. "The Krauts kin spot this jeep from there."

"Ah, the Krauts ain't gonna waste no ammo on one friggin' jeep! Anyway, they're all asleep this time o'day. G'wan, take 'em up there."

"Screw you," the driver said. "You kin show 'em the way. Battalion S-2 expects me back at headquarters, an' I'm already late."

So Rohan and I unloaded our packs and the mortar, and said good-bye to the nervous driver, who backed the jeep, turned around, and took off down the hill in a cloud of dust. After a minute the grimy GI came up out of the cellar carrying his M1 rifle and wiping lather off his face with a towel.

"Follow me," he said grumpily.

VETERAN INFANTRYMAN GREETS US AT THE FRONT

And that was how Rohan and I arrived at that smashed-up little front-line village on the ridge. We may well have been the first two guys from the 5th Infantry Regiment to get up to the front, but we never did know for sure.

CHAPTER 10

FIRST TIME UNDER FIRE

Sunday, March 11, 1945

In 1945 the tiny Alsatian village on what was called Skyline Drive consisted of no more than one or two dozen stone houses and barns, most without roofs. To this day I still am not sure of the name of that village. From the map and text in my tattered copy of *The History of the U.S. Army 71st Infantry Division,* and from an entry in my little pocket notebook, I know only that the village was not far south of a town called Lemberg. This was where the 2d Battalion CP was said to be located. I was able to see Lemberg in the distance, down on the slope of a lower ridge to the north.

My old 1969 Rand McNally atlas shows a tiny village called Goetzenbruck about a mile south of Lemberg, and that could have been the name of it. The larger town of Bitche, close to the German border and the Siegfried Line fortifications, lay just a few more miles north of our ridgetop village.

This little village had just one street running along the skyline, and all of its houses except the first one where the jeep had dropped us off were in a line, facing each other, on both sides of the road, which ran slightly uphill to the right, or east, from where the jeep dropped us off.

At the third house up the street, on the left, the grimy GI turned us over to the weapons platoon sergeant of the company we were to relieve. The back room of that house had a sand-bagged window through which the crew of a .30-caliber light machine gun looked out over a field that sloped down to a ditch a few hundred yards away. On a slight rise beyond the ditch stood a lone farmhouse, with not a single tree around it. The sergeant said the Krauts sometimes used this house for an observation post. Beyond

OUR FIRST VIEW OF "NO-MAN'S LAND"

the farmhouse the field sloped up to a forest in which, we were told, elements of the German 16th Infantry Division were dug in.

Rohan studied the forlorn-looking farmhouse with his binoculars for a long minute, then handed the glasses to me. It was past noon by the time he and I had seen all we cared to see from the sandbagged machine-gun nest in the window looking out toward the German positions in the forest. The veteran sergeant proposed to show us his other machine-gun position next. I was relieved when Rohan said no thanks, and reminded him we were mortarmen, not machine gunners. He asked to see the company's three mortar positions and explained that our primary job as G Company's advance party was to get set up and copy his mortar section's map of likely targets and avenues of approach on which we might have to fire if the Krauts launched an attack during the relief operation that night.

"Well, I'll tell ya," the sergeant drawled apologetically, "my mortar guys don't even have no map. Doubt if they could read one if they did, 'cause they're all replacements. All they got is a list of aim points."

He went on to explain that the mortars usually fired only during the daytime, when the observers could see the targets, watch the rounds hit, and adjust fire. At night, he said, they had never fired anything more than a few illumination flares. For that, they used aiming stakes, azimuth offsets, and a list of preselected aim points with known ranges from the mortar positions. If an OP (observation post) thought they heard a Kraut patrol, they simply called for a flare and gave the aim point number.

Asked about communications, he pointed to a telephone on the floor behind the sandbagged window and said all the OPs were tied in to the mortar section and company CP by phone. Looking at Rohan's walkie-talkie radio, he said that for security reasons they were under orders never to use voice radio unless the phone lines were out. "Too many English-speaking Krauts listening in," he explained. Then he asked if we had any more questions before he sent us across the street to his mortar section.

How relieved I was when Rohan said no. I had many unanswered questions but figured this was not a good time to ask. I couldn't wait to get away from that room facing the ominous German-occupied forest. I imagined that any minute now an 88 shell would come screaming through the narrow window.

With that, the sergeant asked us our names again, then picked up the phone, turned the crank, asked for somebody, and said, *"Well, wake him up, dammit!"* After a wait he said, "Listen, I'm sending two mortar guys from the 5th over to ya. They got their own mortar with 'em. Guy in charge is a Sergeant Rohan. Show 'em the target list and the ammo in the shed. If they wanna use your aiming stakes, move one of your tubes outta the way an' let 'em set their mortar up in its place."

After he hung up, we nodded good-bye to the four or five other men in the room, none of whom had said a word. The sergeant led us back out through the roofless front room and pointed to another smashed house across the road. It had a low stone wall piled with sandbags in front of a small shed. We saw two helmeted GIs motion us toward a gate by the corner of the house to the left of the wall. I hesitated a bit before following Rohan across the exposed road. Then I ran in a crouch, one hand holding on to my helmet and the other holding the strap of the 60mm mortar slung from my shoulder. By the time I reached the gate, one of the GIs had already ushered Rohan into the house through a tarp hung over the doorway.

Just then I heard the sharp *crack* of an explosion a short distance up the street, and the other GI and I turned to see a few roof tiles clatter down onto the pavement. Seconds later there was another loud *crack*, and a puff of smoke rose from the roof of another partially destroyed house.

"Kraut mortars, Sarge," the GI said as Rohan and a staff

A DASH ACROSS THE ROAD UNDER MORTAR FIRE

sergeant came out of the house. I lurched toward them through the gate with what must have been a terrified look on my face. Rohan told me to set the mortar down and come inside; then he and the staff sergeant went back into the house.

"Don't worry, Mac," the GI said as I set the mortar down. "Them little forty-millimeter Kraut mortars can't hurt ya unless they hit a lot closer'n that! One hit about ten yards from me once an' I didn't get a scratch. First time you been up?"

I nodded wordlessly and swallowed, then followed him into the safety of the house, hoping no one would notice I was shaking. Those two mortar rounds were my initiation to combat— my baptism of fire.

The semidark room was the only one in the house with a

solid ceiling. The walls were of thick stone, and the doors to the smashed part of the house had been boarded over. To the right of the tarp-covered entrance was one small glassless window fitted with a blackout curtain that had been pulled aside to let in some light. Rohan sat with the staff sergeant at a small, rough-hewn table beneath this window.

While they talked, I was invited to join several scruffy mortarmen who were opening cartons of K rations at another table. When they saw me pull two C ration cans from my field jacket pocket, I was bombarded with offers to trade. I was not very hungry, so when they explained that they had subsisted on K rations for a month and were sick of them, I agreed to trade all six of my C ration cans for three K ration boxes.

K rations were packed in a rectangular cardboard box coated with wax. The box was just a bit smaller than a carton of cigarettes. One advantage K rations had over C rations was that the box could be burned to heat water in a canteen cup. One such box served one man as one meal; hence each man was issued three boxes per day. Each carton contained a small can of meat and vegetables, or ham and eggs, or cheese; a package of rectangular crackers; a packet of instant coffee, cocoa, or lemonade; a small bar of semisweet hard chocolate that tasted like sawdust; three cigarettes in a small packet—usually the hated Old Gold brand; maybe three sticks of chewing gum; and a book of matches.

C rations came in cans—two per man per meal, or six cans per day. One can contained either hash with potatoes (not bad), or a vegetable-beef stew (also not bad), or ham and eggs (awful). The other can contained six or eight round crackers; a packet of instant coffee, cocoa, or lemonade; and maybe a few pieces of hard candy. C ration aficionados preferred them to K rations only because C rations were more filling.

While the veteran mortarmen of the 100th Infantry Division and I ate our lunch, they explained the setup. Just outside the entryway was the dilapidated shed where the mortar ammunition was stored. One of the company's three 60mm mortars was emplaced in front of this shed, close to the sandbagged wall. The other two mortars were in similar sandbagged emplacements behind the shed.

As we were eating, I suddenly felt the beginnings of diarrhea and asked them where they had their latrine.

"Used to be a shithouse out back," one of them said, "but it got a direct hit so we dug us a trench. C'mon, I'll show ya."

I followed him out the doorway and around the rear corner of the house to a well-worn path leading past the shed in which the mortar ammunition was stored, then to a pile of stinking garbage swarming with flies. To the right of the path was the newly dug latrine trench, and beyond that was a stack of splintered boards that I could see had once been an outhouse. My companion sensed that I wanted to be alone and turned to leave, but at that moment we both saw a beady-eyed rat watching us from the top of the garbage pile.

"Don't move, Mac," he said. "I'll get that son of a bitch!" With that he pulled his .45 from its holster, snapped off the safety, and took aim at the brazen rat. I jumped when he pulled the trigger.

"Missed, dammit!" he said in disgust as the rat ran off. An angry voice from somewhere inside the shed called, "Hey, knock that off over there, will ya? Ya wanna wake up the Krauts?"

"Don't pay him no attention," my companion whispered as he waved at the shed. "That guy's a new replacement, an' he's only an acting squad leader. Kraut mortar damn near got him yesterday, an' he's nervous."

"He's not the only one," I mumbled.

"Yeah. Well, Mac, there's the latrine. See ya later."

Feeling the sharp cramps in my gut and the cold sweat on my forehead, I dropped my pants in a rush and squatted down astride the narrow latrine trench, legs trembling, breathing through my mouth to avoid the stench. I squatted there for a long time, growing weaker with each spasm and more panicky each minute as I imagined getting hit by a mortar shell with my pants down.

When I finally returned to the house, Rohan and the staff sergeant were gone. They had been called to the company CP for a meeting, leaving word for me to stay put and take it easy until they returned. The veteran mortarmen clearly wanted to talk, so for the next hour or two I listened with interest to their stories of combat—some of them so wild I began to suspect that they were putting me on.

Twice I excused myself to go back out to the latrine, and when they were talked out at last, I unrolled my sleeping bag in a corner and went to sleep. Miserable as I was, I looked forward to that night, when the rest of G Company's mortarmen would arrive and I could tell them my own story of my first day in combat.

The 100th Division GIs woke me when Rohan and their sergeant returned, and Johnny and I spent an hour setting up our mortar and learning how to use their numbered list of aim points. It was a simple system, but I found it hard to concentrate, as I was so exhausted and dehydrated from frequent trips to the latrine.

I was not in the least hungry that night, but I had an unquenchable thirst. I sat guard by the mortar for two hours until Rohan relieved me, then I went inside and refilled my canteen from a bucket of water we had been assured was drinkable.

Someone said the water came from a well up the road in an exposed area between two houses, and cautioned me that whoever drank the last of it had to fetch the next bucket. On this note I crawled into my corner to sleep again. Just before midnight, Rohan shook me awake and said the rest of G Company was coming up the road.

With a shuffle of boots and whispered curses, the tired G Company mortar section stumbled one by one through the gate between the house and the sandbagged wall where I stood by the mortar. Most of the 100th Division GIs had left, taking their three mortars with them, but they left one of their squad leaders and a gunner to help Rohan and me show our other two squads where to set up their tubes behind the shed.

So ended my first day in combat on the actual front line.

Chapter 11

FIRST FIRE MISSIONS

Monday, March 12, 1945

There must have been some starlight or moonlight; otherwise I cannot imagine how we could have managed to get the other two mortars set up without using the hooded flashlights carried by each squad leader and gunner. It was decided that two of our three mortars would be manned by two men each, in two-hour shifts, ready to fire flares if called for. Hatley and I would stand our squad's first watch, followed by Decker and Vincent.

Rohan led the others into the house through the blackout curtains formed by an outer and an inner tarp. He and his buddy, Sgt. Ken Bailey of the 2d Squad, came outside shortly with SSgt. Morton Cree—our mortar section leader—and crossed the road to the weapons platoon CP and machine-gun nest from which we had had our first look at no-man's-land.

For the next two hours Waitus Hatley and I shivered and whispered in the cold night air. After the last squad of the 100th Infantry Division riflemen came tramping down the road past our sandbagged wall, I told Hatley all about my first day in combat. I told him about the jeep ride, the machine-gun nest across the road, the Kraut mortars that had given me such a fright, the rat on the garbage pile out in back by the latrine, and some of the hard-to-believe stories the departed 100th Division GIs had told me.

When I asked him about the night march the rest of the company had made up the hill, he said it was so dark and steep it took four hours to go less than four miles. And he allowed as how I was damn lucky to have ridden up in the jeep. I agreed. Of all the men in the 3d Mortar Squad, Hatley was my favorite. Unlike Decker (a glum little guy a few years older than I), or Vincent (somewhat of a smart mouth), Hatley was always good-natured, and his odd name and Alabama accent tickled me.

Shortly before he and I were to be relieved, the stillness of the night was shattered by a burst of gunfire from the direction of the lone farmhouse in the field northeast of our village.

"*Burp gun!*" I croaked, remembering the distinctive *brrrp* sound of the German Schmeisser machine pistol we had been taught to recognize during training at Fort Benning. Almost immediately we heard the field phone inside our house buzz, and whoever was on phone guard answered in a hoarse whisper.

A moment later Rohan hurried across the road, carrying his rifle, flashlight, and raincoat. He squatted down next to me and whispered, breathlessly, "*Second Platoon wants a flare a hundred yards in front of their OP! Quick!*"

With Hatley holding the raincoat over our heads, Rohan switched on his hooded flashlight and flipped open his little notebook to the list of stake numbers and target aim points for each stake. In less time than it takes to tell it, he had given me stake number, azimuth, and range. I had shifted the mortar's bipod legs while he aimed his light at the designated stake. I held my breath and tried to keep my hands from shaking as I squinted into the bubble sight to line it up on the dimly lit stake. Then I cranked in the azimuth, centered the two bubbles, and said, "*Up!*" which means *ready* in the vernacular of mortarmen.

Hatley handed me a flare round, and I pulled its safety pin. Rohan turned off his light, moved aside, and gave the command to fire. I dropped the round into the tube and ducked my head as the round blasted out of the tube with a ringing *thunk*.

Rohan, Hatley, and I all stood up to look over the shoulder-high wall of sandbags, waiting for the flare to burst. Directly across the road from our position was a wide gap between the next house up the hill to the right and the partially destroyed house on the left, where our platoon CP was located. Through this gap we could just make out the dark field to the north, and the pale outline of the lone farmhouse to the northeast. I counted the seconds as we waited.

The 60mm flare rounds were fused to burst at the apex of their trajectory, and that first round I fired in combat burst high over the ditch next to the lone farmhouse. The ditch, farmhouse, and surrounding landscape were all lit up for nearly a minute as the flare floated down to earth, oscillating under its little parachute. I had fully expected to see a line of German infantry advancing across the field toward us, and to see them fall as our machine gun opened up from the house across the road, just like in the movies. But we saw nothing, and when the flare went out, Rohan walked over to the doorway to check with whoever was on the field phone.

After a bit he returned with the word to cease fire. One flare was enough, he said. Then he sent Waitus Hatley into the house to wake up our relief.

It was probably about 4:00 A.M. when Sgt. Ken Bailey came out, followed by Decker, Vincent, and the two mortarmen who were to relieve the crew manning one of the two mortars in back of the shed. I went into the house to get some sleep, leaving Rohan to explain the stakes and aim point list to Bailey and the others.

Still plagued with diarrhea, I woke several times before dawn and had to rush out back to the latrine, careful to give the password to the two nervous GIs of Bailey's squad, who challenged me from behind their emplacement. By my third or fourth trip they knew who it was and began to make jokes, whispering things like, "Jesus Christ, Joy, ya better put a cork in it. Ya sound like an elephant crappin' out there. Krauts kin hear ya all the way to Berlin."

Rohan must have felt sorry for me, as he let me sleep until well after sunrise. I woke up to see Decker, Vincent, Bailey, and several other mortarmen rolled up in their sleeping bags on the stone floor. Hatley sat at the table by the field phone, eating a C ration, but I was unable to stomach the thought of food.

I poured cold water from the bucket into my helmet and splashed some on my face; then I went outside into the sunlight. I will never forget what happened next on that morning of my second day at the front. Had it not been for a lucky oversight on my part, Rohan and I might have killed or wounded some GIs from our own F Company.

The 60mm mortar is simply a small, short-range, muzzle-loading cannon supported by a base plate and bipod legs. It lobs its shells at relatively high angles of fire, from 45 degrees for the lowest trajectory—to give a maximum range of just over a mile—up to 75 or 80 degrees for the highest trajectory, giving a minimum range of about 100 yards. The mortar tube, open at the upper end, is about 30 inches long and 2.5 inches in diameter. The tube's lower end is closed and has a protruding ball-like knob that fits into a socket in the base plate. This socket takes up the shock when a round is dropped into the tube and the mortar fires.

This arrangement permits the tube to be swiveled left or right several degrees, to change the direction or azimuth of fire, and to be elevated or lowered relative to the horizontal to change the range. The key to accurate fire is a removable gunner's sight attached to the left end of a traversing screw mechanism for changing the azimuth. This mechanism is fixed to a collar that clamps around the tube about eight or nine inches below the open mouth. A hand crank on this screw mechanism swings the tube to the left or right. A second hand crank on an elevating screw mechanism, mounted below the tube between the bipod legs, decreases or increases the angle of the tube with the horizontal and hence increases or decreases the range.

The sight has two bubbles, like a carpenter's level—one for lateral leveling and one for longitudinal leveling; these compensate for any slope of the surface on which the base plate and bipod legs are set. Before firing, the gunner must make sure, by using both cranks and by adjusting the length of one of the bipod legs, that both bubbles are centered.

Sounds simple? Well, it isn't. It is not simple because, in addition to centering the bubbles, the gunner must also do something else. He must keep a vertical hairline in the optical sight aligned with an aiming stake or with any other designated vertical object, such as a tree or a fence post. In the most desirable case, the aiming "stake" in front of the mortar lies as close as possible on a line between the mortar and the target. If that is not possible, it is normally the squad leader's job to tell the gunner how many "mils" or "turns" to the right or left of the aiming stake he should turn the crank. Of course, in rare instances when the terrain is flat and the gunner can see the target, he may align the hairline of the sight directly on it, rather than on a stake or a fence post.

So far, so good. But how is the range to the target determined? Usually in the case of larger artillery howitzers or guns, the range is determined by maps, and sometimes by high-power range-finder optics. But the front-line 60mm mortarman has no fancy optics. Squad leaders and gunners have only a pair of binoculars, and it takes practice to use these to estimate target range with any degree of accuracy.

When the mortar is in a defensive position such as ours was, the common practice is to use compasses, maps, binoculars, and the naked eye to select likely aim points—often a dozen or more. The ranges to each point selected are then estimated roughly, and two or three rounds are fired using the standard artillery method known as bracketing. Simply put, this is a trial-and-error technique for adjusting range.

The standard high-explosive (HE) round for the 60mm mortar was eight or nine inches long. It had a conical nose with an impact-type fuse; a cylindrical center section containing the explosive, which is designed to break the casing up into hundreds of lethal fragments; and a tail section containing a cartridge similar to a shotgun shell. When the round slides down the tube, the end of the cartridge strikes a firing pin in the bottom of the tube, and the round goes on its way.

Four tail fins stabilize the round in flight by causing it to spin. Between these fins were four removable "wafers," which served as booster charges to achieve maximum range. Given a range to the target, the gunner consults a range card and tells his assistant gunner what charge to use. "Charge four" means maximum range, in which case all four wafers were left on the round. "Charge zero" means minimum range, in which case all four wafers were removed.

In an ideal textbook situation, as we had practiced many times at Fort Benning, the squad leader's position was on high ground five to twenty yards in front of the mortar, which was typically dug in on the reverse slope of a hill or ridge and thus hidden from enemy view. The squad leader selects his spot so he can observe not only the target and the impact of rounds, but can also see the mortar and relay firing commands by voice or hand signal. The initial range estimate is usually only an approximation, and the wind factor is usually unknown, so the first round may miss the target by many yards in any direction.

And that was the case when I fired a round on Rohan's orders that second morning.

When I joined Johnny at our mortar position behind the sandbags, I noticed a can of oil, a wad of oily rags, and a mortar cleaning rod on the burlap sack where our "ready" rounds of flares and high explosives lay. Rohan explained this cleaning gear by telling me that Decker and Vincent had cleaned the mortar before they came off duty, as we had fired that one flare during the night while they had slept. Happy that I had been spared the cleaning job, I busied myself putting the gear away, then removed the cover from the mouth of the mortar, and ran my finger around the inside of the tube to make sure it had a thin film of rust-preventing oil. While I was thus engaged, Rohan suddenly called out, "Hey, Joy, come take a look at *this!*"

He was standing with his elbows resting on the sandbag wall, his binoculars raised. He handed me the glasses and said, "Look, there's a Kraut watchin' us from the window of that farmhouse."

I focused the glasses and, sure enough, there *was* a figure that was visible in the window of the farmhouse through the gap between the two houses across the road.

"You're right," I said. "That sure looks like a Kraut to me."

"Let's put some rounds on him," Rohan said. "The mortar is still lined up on the stake we used for the flare last night." He gave me the range and offset azimuth, and told me to fire one HE round when ready.

Without hesitation I knelt by the mortar, checked to make sure the sight was focused on the stake, made a slight adjustment to level the bubbles, cranked in the offset, and took the range card from my shirt pocket to check the charge number. I don't remember what charge I used, but when Rohan gave the fire order I quickly pulled the safety pin on a round of HE, dropped it into the tube, ducked, and turned my head away to avoid the muzzle blast.

Then I reached for another round and waited. About ten seconds later I heard the telltale *karrump* of the explosion in the distance.

I looked up at Rohan, who lowered his binoculars and said, "That was over and to the right. Up two turns, left one turn, and fire another."

I made the elevation and traverse adjustments, then fired another round. This time I stood up to watch, so I saw the second shell burst well beyond and to the right of the farmhouse, almost at the edge of the forest. Rohan scowled at me. "*Shit, Joy,*" he swore, "that was even farther over, and way the hell off to the right! Goddammit, I said *up*, not *down*! And I told you

PREPARING TO FIRE AT AN ENEMY OUTPOST

left, not *right*! Now go *up* four turns and *left* two turns and fire another one!"

It was then that I knew something was wrong. I looked at the mortar and saw immediately what had happened. The clamping collar was loose, so that each time the mortar was fired, the collar slipped up on the tube, increasing the range and affecting the azimuth. Now it was I who began to swear. "Goddamn it to hell, Johnny," I exploded, "whoever cleaned this mortar forgot to tighten the clamping collar!"

In fewer than five seconds I had reset and locked the clamping collar, and within half a minute had realigned the sight and fired a third round. I stood up again, and this time we saw the shell burst just to the left of the house.

"That's better," Rohan said. "Half turn right, and fire another." Feeling that my reputation as G Company's best mortar gunner was restored, I carefully cranked in a half turn to the right and fired the fourth round. This time we saw pieces fly off of the farmhouse roof, and several men came running out.

"*Another half turn right, and fire three for effect!*" Rohan practically screamed.

But before I could fire again, we heard an angry voice coming up the road from the company CP, hollering, "*Cease fire, goddammit, cease fire! That's a patrol from F Company out there!*" It was our red-faced company commander, Captain Herbert Neal, and was he ever mad as he ran up to our position.

It is a wonder that both Rohan and I were not busted to buck private as a result of this foul-up, but all that happened was that he was called down to the CP later that morning, given a chewing out, and told how lucky we were that we hadn't wounded or killed anyone. I swore that from then on I would *always* check the clamping collar before firing, and I admonished Decker and the others of the squad to do the same.

CHAPTER 12

FIRST CASUALTIES AND CLOSE CONTACTS WITH THE ENEMY

Tuesday, Wednesday, and Thursday, March 13, 14, and 15, 1945

G Company's first casualty was John V. Krumrine, a buck sergeant from one of our three rifle platoons. He was shot by one
of his own trigger-happy men as he was leading a patrol out in
no-man's-land sometime before midnight on Tuesday, March
13, 1945.

That day was my third at the front. It had passed by quietly
until sometime in the afternoon, when Johnny Rohan decided
on his own initiative to take a firsthand look at a German position closest to the village—and invited me to come along. The
position in question was on our right flank, on the edge of the
forest a few yards from the last house on the ridge to the east.

This idea was not at all to my liking. It goes without saying
that I would have much preferred to stay in the relative safety of
the thick-walled stone house where we mortarmen spent most of
our time when not standing guard outside by our mortars. There
were to be many times in the coming days and weeks when I felt

like refusing to take what I thought were stupid and unnecessary chances—and this was one of them.

The fear of being regarded as a coward was a powerful incentive, so I reluctantly put on my gear and followed Rohan up the road. We stayed close to the smashed houses on our left, crossing the gaps between them on the run. I took note of the village well and its ancient-looking hand pump in one of the exposed gaps. We passed two or three more houses, then came to the end of the paved road in front of the last house—a large two-story structure with a partially destroyed and fire-blackened roof. To the left of this house were remnants of a few shell-shattered trees, and to the right, where the pavement ended, a narrow dirt track disappeared down the slope through an orchard. As we would learn a few nights later, this dirt road and orchard were sown with German land mines.

Technical Sergeant Nero—a New York Italian who was sergeant of one of our rifle platoons—met us at the door to this last house. We picked our way through broken glass and pieces of furniture, then climbed a makeshift ladder through a trapdoor to the atticlike second story. Nero explained that this was not only an observation post (OP) for his rifle platoon but also for the artillery forward observer (FO) who was assigned to G Company from the 105mm howitzer battalion that supported the 5th Infantry Regiment.

The attic had sandbagged windows below what remained of its steeply sloped roof. Looking through a shell hole, I could see the woods about fifty yards to the east. A rifleman with a Browning Automatic Rifle (BAR) stood peering through another shell hole, while the FO—a businesslike young artillery lieutenant—sat on the floor next to a field telephone, looking at a map with a buck sergeant I assumed to be his assistant.

Nero—in whose rifle platoon I had once been assigned for a few days at Fort Benning before my transfer to our weapons platoon—introduced us to the FO and his sergeant, and asked them to show us their map and its various aim points. He jokingly referred to us as "G Company's light artillery." This is, in fact, what we infantry mortarmen proudly called ourselves.

CLOSE LOOK AT THE ENEMY FROM AN OP

While the two artillerymen explained their targeting system to Rohan, pointing out the red-and-blue grease pencil symbols on their topographic map, the rifleman with the BAR called me over. He handed me his binoculars and stood aside to let me look out through a large shell hole in the steeply sloped roof. Shafts of light from the late-afternoon sun penetrated several yards into the nearby edge of the German-held forest, but I could see no sign of life. After a quick look I handed the glasses back to him and asked if he had seen any Krauts yet.

He shook his head no, then said, "We kin sure hear 'em at night, though, 'specially when the wind's blowin' this way. Sounds like the rattlin' of pans and mess kits. Last night we even heard a horse snortin', and one of our guys who speaks German swears he heard some of 'em bitchin' about their lousy chow. Must bring it up in a wagon after dark."

As I was pondering this, wondering if the Krauts got fed hot food at night, the rifleman with the BAR raised his binoculars and looked out through his shell hole again. Suddenly he exclaimed, "Hey! Whaddya know! *There's* a *Kraut* now! Diggin' hisself a hole behind that tree! Hey, Sergeant Nero! Lieutenant! Take a look at that guy!"

I peeked through a smaller shell hole and, sure enough, I saw my first live German soldier. He was half hidden behind the trunk of a pine tree about fifty yards from the house and apparently was digging a foxhole. He stopped once to look up in our direction and I instinctively ducked, but when I looked again he had nonchalantly resumed his digging.

Nero, Rohan, and the two artillerymen were also peering out through holes in the slanted roof, and the BAR man asked Nero if he should "take a shot at that stupid asshole." Nero shook his head, and the lieutenant said it wouldn't be worth it to reveal the existence of the OP. Then he said that there probably were more Krauts hidden nearby, and he'd better call Captain Neal.

The next several minutes were ridiculously comical. It seemed that the question of whether to fire a salvo of artillery at one poor German soldier had to be referred all the way up the chain of command—maybe as far as division, or Eisenhower himself!

First, Captain Neal told the lieutenant he was being "put through to battalion."

After a long wait, the young officer shook his head and said, "Now they're putting me through to regiment." And finally, after a longer wait, he turned to us and said, "Regiment says to fire a salvo at that Kraut if he's still there and if we're sure of the coordinates. They're worried that he might be too close to us for comfort if there is a short round."

But by this time it was too late. The German was no longer in sight. The lieutenant dutifully reported this fact, and no artillery was fired.

Before we left the OP, Rohan spent some time showing Nero and the artillerymen the location of our mortar on the map, and going over our list of target aim points and ranges in an attempt to correlate them with the artillery's preselected target coordinates. It was decided that we should add a few targets to our list, but I had left my list with Decker. Rohan tore a blank page from his notebook and told me to write down the ranges and compass bearings as given to me by the artillery sergeant. The sergeant calculated these from his map by using a straightedge and a circular template graduated in mils and degrees.

It was after sundown when Rohan and I returned to our mortar position. Sergeant Bailey was waiting at the gate with news of a meeting of all NCOs at the company CP, so I was left in temporary charge when they left. Just as I was telling the others the story of our afternoon adventure, Rohan called me on the field phone, told me to leave Decker in charge, and hurry down to the CP with the new target list I had copied.

It was dark when I arrived at the company CP and opened the wrought iron gate with a clang. The door to the house opened and out came 1st Sgt. Carl Anderson, looking grimy as usual. I could see he was nervous and mad.

"Hi, Top," I greeted him as I pulled the folded target list from my field jacket pocket. The gate clanged shut behind me. "Here's a target list Rohan wanted," I said. "Is he in there?"

"*Shh*, for chrissake!" Anderson sputtered in a hoarse whisper. "Doncha know the Krauts got ears? Keep yer voice down and don't never let that gate slam like that again!"

I heard fear in his voice and realized that he was, as we all used to say, *scared shitless*. He grabbed the folded piece of paper, told me to wait outside, and disappeared into the house. Shortly thereafter, our mortar squad leaders came out, followed by several other NCOs. One of these must have been Sergeant Krumrine, who was killed later that night while leading his patrol into the woods where we had seen the German digging his foxhole.

The morning of our fourth day at the front—Wednesday, March 14—was quiet except for a constant rumble of distant artillery to the north. I was in the house, listening to someone's rumor that the Seventh Army had entered Germany, had taken Saarbrücken, and was using its big guns in preparation for an attack through the Siegfried Line, to help Patton's Third Army cut off the Germans still west of the Rhine in the Saar Basin.

Based on this rumor, a few optimists in the group argued that the war would probably end before the green 71st Division could be called on to join the final offensive. They even went so far as to argue that most of the Krauts in the woods northeast and east of our village had probably left the night before, in the rush to escape across the Rhine.

I reminded them of the German I had seen digging a foxhole the previous afternoon, but they discounted this. They argued that not one enemy patrol had probed our position in the three days we had been on the line, nor had any prisoners been taken, nor had we sustained any serious artillery fire. Not true, I said, reminding them of the German mortar fire the day Rohan and I had arrived. On that note, I went out to our mortar.

Moments later, as if the enemy were letting us know he was still there, I heard a *swish,* then a big shell exploded with a loud *crack* on the road near the well. I heard the *whizz-tink-tink* of shrapnel bounding off of stone walls, and I ducked down behind the sandbags next to Decker and Vincent. One of them said,

"Shit, man, that must have been an eighty-eight! We better get inside in case there's more coming!"

I could think of nothing I'd rather do, and was about to agree when I saw Johnny Rohan come dashing across the road toward us from the weapons platoon CP, where he and the other two squad leaders had been called to a meeting. After he made sure no one had been hit, he told us to keep our heads down; then he dashed back across the road to the CP.

Several minutes passed. No more shells arrived. We had just begun to relax when we heard a high-powered plane coming from the east. We looked up and saw the unmistakable shape of an American P-47 Thunderbolt fighter, recognizable from its large cowl and elliptical wings. As we watched, it suddenly banked north—and we could see black crosses on its wings and a swastika on its tail!

Speechless, we watched it go into a dive and saw a bomb drop as it pulled out and turned back to the east. Seconds later, we felt the concussion. That afternoon we learned from someone that the P-47 was one of four known to have been captured intact by the Germans, and that its bomb had just missed our battalion CP in Lemberg. The same source reported that the four captured P-47s had strafed the 66th Infantry Regiment the preceding day, killing two men. After the war, I read in our 71st Division history book that those two men were the division's first casualties from enemy action.

That afternoon those of us not on duty sat in the safety of our stone house debating our chances of surviving the war, the immorality of German pilots flying captured P-47 Thunderbolts, and how badly whoever had shot Krumrine the night before must feel. Having exhausted these subjects, someone—probably Rohan—told me I was beginning to stink, and I was embarrassed. I had not shaved or had so much as a sponge bath for days, so I promised to rectify the situation.

A few others in the group, Rohan and Bailey included, had

already shaved and bathed using hot water courtesy of the enterprising Johnny Rohan. Earlier that morning he had scrounged a fire-blackened washbasin and supervised the digging of a rock-lined fire pit in a sheltered spot in back of the house. Then he had split up some of the splintered wood planks that had once been the outhouse and fetched the first two buckets of water from the exposed well up the road. After his sponge bath, Rohan let it be known that anyone else who wanted hot water for a shave and a bath was welcome as long as he split his own firewood and fetched his own water from the well.

Remembering the shell that had hit the road that morning, I had held off going up to the well. To reduce the risk, I planned to wait until dusk. But I knew that the fire in the pit had to be put out before dark, so I forced myself to make the trip in broad daylight. Going up the road with empty buckets wasn't so bad because I could run in a crouch. But pumping that squeaking handle to fill the buckets seemed to take forever, and the trip back down the road was made at a slow trot to avoid spillage. Oh, how badly I wanted to drop those full buckets and run back to safety!

It is remarkable what a clean shave and a change of underwear after a warm sponge bath can do for a combat infantryman's sagging morale. My diarrhea was gone at last, so that night I wolfed down my C rations and, for the first time since coming up to the front, I slept soundly for several hours. I forgot all about the war and probably dreamed of Rita Hayworth—a favorite pinup girl made famous by a sexy picture in *Life* magazine.

Awakened by the *thunk-thunk-thunk* of our mortars firing in rapid succession, I looked at my watch and saw that Hatley and I weren't due to relieve Decker and Vincent for another hour, so when the mortars ceased firing, I went back to sleep. When Rohan woke me up at 2:00 A.M. he explained that two of our three mortars had fired about a dozen rounds into the woods east of the village after a lookout in the OP we had visited reported hearing sounds of horses and mess kits again. As was usually the case with unobserved fire, no one knew for sure if the mortars had hit anything.

That afternoon, our fifth day at the front, G Company captured its first prisoner. Hatley and I were outside by our mortar when Sergeant Nero ran the Kraut down the road past our sandbagged position. I noted the look of terror on that German's ashen face as Nero jabbed him with the bayonet on his M1 and said, *"Schnell, you son of a bitch!"*

Just after dark we received the welcome news that our mess sergeant was bringing a jeep and a trailerload of hot food up to the company CP. Each platoon was given a schedule for sending a third of its men down, each man to carry three mess kits, to bring the rations back up to the front-line houses. Typically, the mortar section was scheduled last, and Rohan volunteered our five-man squad to fetch the rations for the other two mortar squads.

When we joined a line of riflemen shuffling toward the jeep and trailer parked in the dark by a wall next to the CP, we saw the German prisoner sitting with his back against the wall, facing a guard with a bayonet on his rifle. Squatting next to the POW was our German-speaking platoon sergeant, Alfred Feltman, who was asking him questions.

"Hey, Al," Rohan called. "Whadja find out? Is that Kraut one of those SS troopers?"

Recognizing us in the dark, Feltman stood up, came over, and said, "No, he's just a poor old farmer who's been in the Wehrmacht for only a week. He was drafted as a cook."

Feltman told us that the prisoner had decided to surrender after our mortars had killed his horse and wounded several men in a chow line the previous night. He claimed that all of the surviving Germans in the woods except him had pulled out, because his entire regiment had been ordered to withdraw.

A chorus of mortarmen exclaimed "No shit?" and "How about that!" and "I don't believe it," until our nervous old topkick, Carl Anderson, came rushing back along the line from somewhere in the dark and told us to shut up.

"Krauts got ears, too!" he hissed. "Ya want 'em to drop mortars on this chow line, like ya done to theirs?"

We shook our heads and fell silent, but when old Top walked away, Feltman grinned and whispered that if the prisoner was telling the truth, there were no Krauts left within earshot. Even so, he said, we should keep our voices down. I thought that if the withdrawal story was true, we would probably be ordered to attack soon—a prospect I dreaded. I speculated that the reason we were getting hot rations was that we were going on the offensive.

By the time we returned to our house and the other mortarmen had been handed their mess kits, the beef stew was cold. There was a lot of bitching about this as we ate in the dim candlelight, and more bitching when we tried to clean our greasy mess kits in cold water. Someone sent a detail up the road to the well for more water, and Hatley and I went outside to watch them from behind our sandbagged mortar position. Suddenly, all hell broke loose.

It began with a long *brrrrrrrrrrrrp* of rapid machine-gun fire from somewhere in the dark gap between the two houses across the road. This was followed by several *brrrp brrrps* from somewhere behind us. Slugs ricocheted off the walls of our house and others up the road. They went *zeeoww zeeoww,* and we ducked.

One of our own slower-firing light machine guns replied with a *pop-pop-pop-pop-pop,* and a BAR chimed in with a more deliberate *pow-pow-pow.* In that moment of terror I would have given anything for a BAR or at least an M1 rifle, but I crouched behind the sandbags, armed with nothing but two hand grenades and my .45-caliber automatic pistol. Waitus Hatley was not much better off; he had his two grenades and a carbine.

The German machine gun fired another long burst, answered this time by the BAR and several M1 rifles firing from houses across the road. Then all was quiet.

A moment later, Sergeants Rohan and Bailey came running out of our house with their M1s, followed by two or three mortarmen with carbines. Rohan crouched down next to me and gasped that Kraut patrols were reportedly trying to infiltrate the village from the rear by sneaking through the hedges in back of the houses on our side of the road, while another Kraut patrol made a diversion with its machine gun from the field north of the village.

I asked Rohan if we should fire some mortar flares, but he whispered that the patrols were too close to us. Then he said that he and Bailey and the men with them would go out back to reconnoiter and set up a guard by the latrine. His parting words were that Hatley and I should sit tight and watch the road.

Numb with fear, I rechecked my .45 to make sure there was a round in the chamber. The equally frightened Hatley chambered a round in his carbine. Then we placed our hand grenades within reach on top of the sandbags and settled down to keep watch.

Minutes passed in silence, then the German machine gun fired again with a long *brrrrrrrrrrrrp*. We ducked again, but this time we could tell from the sound that the firing was not aimed in our direction. We peeked over the sandbags and saw tracers zip from right to left in the gap between the houses across the road, then fly up and disappear into the night sky. After a few desultory M1 rifle shots from somewhere, the firing ceased.

In the ensuing silence I heard the sound of boots running down the road from the right. I snapped off the safety of my automatic and picked up a grenade. Just as we recognized the runner as one of the men who had been sent up to the well for water, I heard a movement in the shed behind us. Panicked, I turned my head to see a shadowy figure emerge through the half-open door to the shed. I was about to pull the pin on the grenade when I recognized Johnny Rohan.

TEN MINUTES OF TERROR AT OUR MORTAR POSITION

"Jesus Christ, John!" I croaked angrily. "You scared the shit out of me! I thought you were a German!" It was then that I remembered the mortar ammunition stored in the shed, and thought, *Joy, if you had thrown that grenade, all three of us might have been blown to bits!*

Hatley told me later that he, too, had thought Rohan was a Kraut and had nearly shot him with his carbine. I doubt if our intrepid squad leader ever realized how close he had come to being shot by his own men. There were no more reports of enemy patrols that night, and so ended my fifth day in combat—Thursday, March 15, 1945.

CHAPTER 13

THROUGH THE MINEFIELD TO THE SIEGFRIED LINE

Friday, March 16, through Thursday, March 22, 1945

The first mail to reach us at the front was brought up to the company CP by the mess sergeant before dawn on Friday, March 16. At about midmorning we got the word via field phone to send two men down to pick up our mail along with our daily issue of C rations. I had just finished writing my first letter home since arriving at the front six days earlier; I wanted to get it sent off, so I volunteered to go along with another GI from our mortar section. Rarely did mail call bring me fewer than two or three letters, sometimes more. But on this sunny morning I was disappointed to receive none at all.

In the last letter I had received—delivered to Camp Old Gold just before we left for the front—my mother had written that the papers were full of news of a "big push" and said that the 71st Division had been mentioned. Naturally, she asked if I could say whether we had been in it. On my last leave I had told my parents of a code I would use to let them know if and when our division had been committed to combat. And so it was that the last paragraph of the letter I took down to the company CP that morning read: "*I was surprised to hear from Ned York—you remember him, Mother, the guy who told you he was going to be a Jewish chaplain in the army—he's a relative of Kate Myrick. Said he missed the big push, but that he was in the fighting.*"

The code name "Ned" was, of course, my first name spelled backward without the "a"; York was the name of the Denver street we had once lived on; Kate Myrick was the maiden name of my long-dead maternal grandmother; and I had once joked that, if drafted, I might change my religion to Jewish and try to avoid combat by becoming a Jewish chaplain. I had figured that our platoon leader, Lieutenant Tyler, was too dumb to suspect my code when he censored my letter. Dumb or not, he let it go through.

I was torn between not trying to tell them we were in combat, which might worry them needlessly, and trying to warn them that they might any day receive a dreaded telegram. I tried to ease their minds by ending the letter on an upbeat note. "*I am O.K., a lot better off than lots of guys in Europe, and happy as possible*"—not exactly true, as most of the time so far I was too scared to be happy.

That night the low layers of clouds all along the front glowed with artificial moonlight created by the reflection of searchlights deployed somewhere to our rear. No Kraut patrols dared to expose themselves in the eerie half light that bathed the fields between our ridge and the German-held forest. Except for a few flurries of distant small-arms fire, the night passed quietly.

The next day, Saturday, March 17, it was rumored once again that the Germans were retreating to their Siegfried Line, and several times we heard the *swish-swish-swish* of salvos of our artillery passing overhead, followed by the *crump-crump-crump* of the exploding shells to the north and east. Late that afternoon our squad leaders returned from a meeting, bringing the unwelcome word that G Company was to attack at dawn the next morning!

In preparation for this attack, all company weapons were to open up at 5:00 A.M. and fire for two solid minutes. In those two minutes our orders were to fire half of the estimated 360 rounds of mortar ammunition stored in the shed. Each mortar was given four aim points and was to fire fifteen rounds at each aim point, at the maximum rate of thirty rounds per minute. We would then pack up, each squad's two ammunition bearers carrying six rounds in their vestlike canvas pouches. We were to follow our attacking rifle platoons into the forest to the east.

I wondered why this preparatory fire was needed if the Krauts had pulled out, as rumored, but it was nevertheless comforting to think that as a result of our mortar fire, any diehards the Germans left behind to hold up our advance might surrender without a fight. And so, while it was still light, we spent some time adjusting aiming stakes, preparing fire plans, and bringing more mortar ammunition from the shed.

The containers in which our 60mm mortar rounds were delivered to the front were heavy cardboard cylinders, about three feet long and six or seven inches in diameter. Each container held nine rounds sealed in smaller individual cardboard tubes. As the predawn fire plan called for our three mortars to fire a total of 180 rounds, we unpacked twenty of the large cylindrical containers. The first few of these we tossed over the sandbagged wall onto a jumbled stack of empties that had been there since the day Rohan and I had come up. At some point they started to roll off of the stack into the road, so we dumped the rest of them behind the shed.

When we finished this chore, those of us who were not scheduled for guard duty went into the house to clean our pistols and carbines and to get some sleep. An hour or two later, word came that there would be no preparatory fire after all. We were told that the veteran 45th Infantry Division, on our right flank, had cleared the forest to within half a mile of our ridgetop village and had requested that we send out a patrol to contact their advance elements. Under this new plan, a squad of engineers would accompany the G Company patrol to clear a path through the minefields, and the rest of the company would follow.

Much to our disgust, we were ordered to repack all of the mortar ammunition we could not carry, for later pickup by trucks from the regimental service company. While our squad leaders went down to the company CP for another briefing, I was left in charge of the repacking. I set Decker, Hatley, and Vincent to work loading individual rounds into the small tubes, while others in the detail brought us the empty larger containers from behind the shed. When I pulled off the lid from one container I was assailed by the stench of fresh human excrement. With a curse, I pulled the lids from two more, only to find that both had been similarly used by whoever had been too lazy to make a trip to the latrine.

"Goddamnit," I whispered, "who crapped in these tubes?" No one from the other two mortar squads admitted it, so I told them they could damn well load their own ammo in their own goddamn crap-filled containers for all I cared. With that, I stood up and reached over the sandbags for the nearest containers in the stack left by the 100th Division mortarmen. But after sticking my hand into several of those old containers, I found that they were full of old dried crap. After more cursing, I found several that had not been used, and we finally finished the job.

At about this time Rohan returned to check on the repacking, told me to be sure to make an accurate count, and then disappeared up the road. Shortly after that, Ken Bailey appeared. He laughed when I told him about the crap in the containers, but I was furious—it had been his squad that had used them. For some reason, Bailey and I had taken an unspoken dislike to one another back at Fort Benning. Perhaps it was because we were in competition for Rohan's friendship. In any case, I found Bailey just a bit too officious for a lowly buck sergeant. That night I gave vent to my feelings when he went into the house to answer the field phone, then called for me. When I came through the blackout curtains into the candlelit room, he excitedly told me that Sergeant Nero was on the line with the news that exploding mines had wounded some of the riflemen and a medic with the patrol that had been sent out earlier. Nero wanted someone to bring up a bucket of water.

"Joy," said Bailey in an officious tone, "get a bucket, take it up the road, fill it at the pump, and bring it on up to the last house where Nero and Rohan are waiting."

"Did Rohan tell you to send me?" I asked.

"No, but since you were up there before, you know the way."

"Bailey," I said, "I take orders from Rohan, and I have to finish counting these rounds we've packed. Send one of your own men, or take it up yourself!"

"Goddamnit, Joy," he exploded, "that's a direct order!"

Fortunately for me, the confrontation ended when our section leader, Staff Sergeant Cree, came into the room with orders to get our gear together and prepare to move out in fifteen minutes. The story Rohan told us later was that two riflemen had been seriously wounded by a mine, that a brave medic had dragged one of them to safety, and then had gone back to help the other rifleman. But both the medic and the second wounded man had been killed outright when another mine exploded.

Sometime after midnight on Sunday, March 18, our mortar section lined up on the dark road behind a squad of riflemen, waiting for the order to move out. In addition to our heavy packs, I carried our squad's mortar tube and folded bipod legs, Decker carried the base plate, and Hatley and Vincent each wore ammunition vests with six mortar rounds apiece. As we waited, a jeep crept slowly up the road from the CP, and we recognized

Captain Neal in the front passenger seat. A few minutes later the jeep returned, empty except for the driver, and the order was passed to move out.

We marched in two columns, one on either side of the road, until we reached the cul-de-sac where the pavement ended in front of the house from which Rohan and I had seen the German digging a foxhole at the edge of the forest. There the columns came to a temporary halt, then merged into a single slow-moving column that wound its way down the dirt trail through the orchard. Partway through the orchard we turned left off the trail onto a narrow path that disappeared into the dark pine forest.

About a hundred yards into the trees we moved past a shadowy figure we recognized as our company executive officer, First Lieutenant Doneski. He whispered a warning to stay on the path between the white tapes marking the lane that had been cleared of mines by the engineers earlier that night.

We had been told that the mines were of the "bouncing betty" type—a much-dreaded antipersonnel mine that consisted of a buried canister of steel pellets that, when set off by stepping on a small exposed trigger, popped up and exploded at knee height.

The tape-marked path zigzagged two hundred or three hundred yards up the slope through the dark forest, then descended, and debouched into a large clearing. Ahead we could hear water burbling, and the path crossed the clearing to a narrow creek, where the tape ended. The column slowed and bunched up as we waded the shallow stream, climbed the bank, and turned left onto a rutted wagon trail. Word was passed back that we were through the minefield and should form a column of twos again, keeping five-yard intervals.

Burdened as I was with at least eighty pounds of equipment, including the mortar tube and my heavy combat pack, I found it hard to keep up with Johnny Rohan. The gap between us grew from five yards to ten, then twenty, as the column left the trail to

NIGHT MARCH THROUGH THE MINEFIELD

climb another open slope that was strewn with fallen logs. I could hear Decker, Hatley, and Vincent huffing and puffing behind me, and by the time word was passed to take a break, we were utterly exhausted. Gasping, I made my way to a dark lump I took to be a log and sat down. I felt a softness and smelled something putrid. Then I saw the shape of a German coal-scuttle helmet nearby and was suddenly horrified to realize that I was sitting on a dead Kraut.

I was careful not to touch the corpse with my hands as I stood up, and then stumbled over to where Rohan sat on a fallen tree.

"Just sat on a goddamn dead Kraut," I laughed noncha-lantly, trying to hide my revulsion. That contact with the first of many dead bodies I would see in the coming days marked the onset of my callous irreverence for all enemy dead—typical, I think, of most combat infantrymen.

We moved out a few minutes later, following another tape-marked trail through another minefield. Finally we halted on a hillside and were told to dig foxholes and bivouac for the rest of the night. Decker and I dug a deep pit for our mortar. That first night in a front-line foxhole it was miserably cold, and when I awoke at dawn, the hillside was covered with dense fog.

When the fog began to burn off at about eight that morning we could just make out a long, open valley below us. Someone said that the valley led north to the Alsatian town of Bitche, and beyond that lay the German border and the Siegfried Line.

We loaded up before noon and moved out again. We hiked all day on a well-worn path that wound through pine forests and crossed several footbridges over deep, narrow ravines. The going was easy, and every hour or so we stopped for a ten-minute break, with a full hour for lunch by a rushing stream in a sunlit clearing.

There were trout in the stream, and I fell asleep dreaming of the many idyllic fishing trips I had taken with my father in the Rocky Mountains. I awoke to the distant sound of artillery and a spattering of small-arms fire, and heard the rasping voice of First Sergeant Anderson shouting, "George Company, on yer feet. We're movin' out!"

Just before sundown we came out of the woods onto the nose of a hill. We could see smoke rising from the valley below. Word was passed to dig in for the night. Luckily, our mortar section found several old foxholes and gun pits in the sector of the perimeter to which we were assigned, so we were spared the chore of digging.

From the empty shell casings, remnants of several bales of hay, and piles of fresh horse manure strewn around the gun pits, it was evident that a horse-drawn battery of German artillery had recently occupied the position. After checking for booby traps, we set up each mortar in a separate gun pit. Decker and I slept together, warm and comfortable, in a two-man foxhole filled with hay, until our squad was awakened to stand guard.

An hour into our guard shift we heard the drone of an airplane, then another and another, and suddenly the sky to the north was filled with strings of orange-yellow tracers floating eastward across the valley floor below. For several minutes we watched the fireworks and listened to the distant *chug-chug-chug* of heavy .50-caliber antiaircraft machine-gun fire. Then all was quiet again.

When it was time for me to wake the mortar squad that was to relieve us on guard, the night was so pitch black that I lost my bearings and couldn't find their foxholes for several minutes. Then, without warning, I stumbled and fell headfirst into one. Its terrified occupant grunted, turned with a muffled curse, and rose up holding a .45 automatic in his hand!

"Don't shoot, for chrissake!" I croaked. "It's me, Joy! Time to go on guard."

To my great relief he lowered the pistol but called me every vile name in the book while I tried to climb out of the hole without falling on him again. It was dark, but from his southern drawl I recognized it was a surly kid named Packard.

At dawn the next morning—Monday, March 19—we moved out in a gently falling rain and hiked down a winding mountain road that descended into the valley to a paved highway leading north to a burning village in the distance. Parked alongside the highway were a few trucks and radio jeeps bearing the insignia of the 71st Division's 564th Field Artillery Battalion, and there was a battery of its heavy 155mm guns deployed in a muddy field nearby. The 155s loosed a salvo just as we marched past, and we jumped at the concussions.

Then from behind us we heard the grinding gears of a truck convoy approaching, and we moved to the shoulders of the highway to let it pass. Led by a jeep with the bumper insignia of the 14th Infantry Regiment—one of our division's two other regiments—the convoy moved slowly past as we slogged along in the rain. The trucks were loaded with troops with whom we exchanged good-natured insults. When the big howitzers fired another salvo, the trucks seemed to accelerate like startled rabbits. They soon disappeared up the road, headed for the smoke rising in the distance.

Just before noon the rain stopped, the sun came out, and word was passed for G Company to take a break in an apple orchard on the outskirts of the burning village. We dropped our packs and settled down under the gnarled old apple trees, whose bare branches were just beginning to bud. I knew that spring was in the air when I heard birds chirping in a nearby hedge. A few men gathered twigs and started small fires to heat their coffee and cans of C rations, but I decided to eat a candy bar, received in trade for a pack of cigarettes. Using my pack as a pillow, I lay down near a tree and closed my eyes, listening to the birds, dreaming of boxes of cookies from home, and wondering if our mail would ever catch up with us now that we were on the move. My reverie was broken by the sudden sound of an incoming artillery shell, followed by a loud *crack!*

The shell hit just across the road from our orchard. Someone shouted to douse the smoking fires and keep spread out, but no more shells came in, and after a minute someone said, "If them Krauts were tryin' ta hit them 155s, their aim is piss poor." And someone else said, "Bastards must be short of ammo if all they can spare is one lousy round."

Shortly after that, a jeep with a trailer came tearing down the road toward us, slowed, and turned into the orchard. Next to the driver sat our grinning company clerk, who hollered "Mail call!" as the jeep and the trailer bounced past us through the trees. There was a near-stampede as those of us within earshot—myself included—jumped up and started running toward the little knot of company headquarters men where the jeep had stopped. But our irate first sergeant barred the way, waving his arms and shouting, "Git back as ya were! Doncha dumb goddamn sojers have any brains? Y'all wanna git wiped out by artillery?"

Old Top had a point, of course. The rule had been drilled into us *never* to bunch up in groups larger than a squad when within range of enemy artillery. So we slunk back to where we had left our packs and waited impatiently, until our mortar section was finally called to get its mail.

According to a letter I wrote the next morning—the first day of spring—that mail call in the apple orchard brought me *two* boxes of food and three letters from my mother. The boxes contained doughnuts, cookies, dates, candy, and nuts, and although one had been mailed three months earlier and was addressed to Fort Benning, I wrote that its contents were still edible. When we moved out later that afternoon, there was no way I could have carried all that stuff in my pack, so it must have been shared on the spot with the others in my squad.

A rumor made the rounds that we were to attack Bitche the next day, and that the Germans had modified the French pillboxes to face south instead of north. As might be expected, someone said that if the rumor was true, taking that town would be a son of a bitch. As it turned out, the 14th Infantry Regiment took the town quickly early the next morning, March 22, with very few casualties. At about ten o'clock that morning our 5th Infantry Regiment—now in division reserve—marched through the town. We were surprised to see no signs of damage to the pillboxes.

We continued to march on to the north, and after a rugged six-hour hike of twenty miles or so, we crossed the border into Germany. Just before dusk we dug foxholes on a hillside near the village of Roppweiler. From that hill we looked down into a long valley, and could see the antitank dragons' teeth of the Siegfried

Line gleaming white in the late-afternoon sun. They looked just like the photographs I had seen in the newspapers, and they stretched for what appeared to be several miles. It was an awesome sight.

The ground was so hard that digging foxholes of any depth was extremely difficult using the small folding shovels or mattock-like picks we carried. Decker had a pick, I had a shovel, and we took turns digging a two-man hole big enough for our mortar.

Although it was not a recommended practice, in training we had been told that hand grenades could be used to help blast out a foxhole when the ground was hard or frozen. The Irish kid we called Shakey Hayes, a member of Sergeant Bailey's Second

DIGGING FOXHOLES OVERLOOKING THE SIEGFRIED LINE

Mortar Squad, decided to try this method. He dug a small hole, then set off a hand grenade in it. We heard the muffled explosion and saw dirt fly up from where Hayes lay prone next to the hole. My first thought was that Hayes had been blown up by a German mine, but he rose with a lopsided grin while several non-coms came running over. Feltman chewed Hayes out mercilessly.

That night a few copies of *Stars and Stripes* reached us, and I read that in the twelve days I had been officially in combat, the U.S. First Army had put a full corps across the Rhine River on a bridge captured at Remagen. The paper also said that Patton's Third Army and Patch's Seventh Army had breached the Siegfried Line at several places in the Saar and were expected to cross the Rhine any day. The Russians were reported to be only two days' march from Berlin!

As we read this good news, most of us were sure that the war would end in a few days or, at most, weeks.

CHAPTER 14

CARNAGE AT PIRMASENS

Friday and Saturday, March 23 and 24, 1945

Friday morning we abandoned our shallow foxholes on the hill overlooking Roppweiler, marched down through the empty village, then turned east on a valley road along the edge of the line of dragon's teeth that stretched as far as the eye could see. We were told that the Germans, in their rush to escape across the Rhine, had abandoned this part of the Siegfried Line, built to protect the southern flank of the Saar region, and that we could expect one or two days of hard marching as part of a general pursuit of the fleeing enemy.

The second day of spring 1945 was sunny and warm, and we bitched at having to walk when truck after truck filled with other companies of our regiment roared past. That afternoon a few rounds of long-range German artillery landed on the barren hills ahead, just to the left of our advancing column. Several times during the day we marched past groups of dejected-looking German prisoners guarded by MPs. We bivouacked that night in a field near the road.

The next morning, Saturday, March 24, showed promise of being another sunny day, but it was also our turn to ride. Just before noon, when our trucks approached the southern outskirts of Pirmasens, we saw several dead Germans in a ditch alongside the road behind a recently cleared log roadblock, and we had our first close look at a few menacing but fire-blackened pillboxes.

Pirmasens was a fair-size city that appeared to have been heavily bombed. Its streets were strewn with rubble, and our trucks had to detour around several craters in front of what remained of a large church, whose twin towers were still standing. Dozens of white sheets and towels signifying surrender hung from windows of nearly every building we passed, and here and there we saw groups of unarmed German soldiers emerge into the sunlit street, their hands in the air; some of them were holding white handkerchiefs.

Once, while we were stopped for some reason, a German family came out of a side street with a cart carrying whatever was left of their belongings. A pitiful-looking old man with a rope over his shoulder was pulling the cart, while several women and small children pushed. We felt especially sorry for one hungry-looking, dirty-faced little girl in a ragged dress, and someone tossed her a pack of chewing gum. But a scowling blond woman in a kerchief knocked it out of her hand and pushed her roughly on down the cobblestone road, leaving the gum in the gutter.

"*Ya Nazi bitch!*" shouted the GI who had thrown the gum, and several of us added a cacophony of insulting jeers. But the woman never looked back. Those were the first enemy civilians I had seen, and as I looked at the smashed buildings I thought, *How they must hate us!* But what did they expect? They or their leaders started the war, not we!

Our own propaganda had taught us to hate all uniformed "Kraut" soldiers, but that moment marked the beginning of my

SAD SCENE—A REFUGEE FAMILY AT PIRMASENS

hatred for *all* adult Germans—a juvenile emotion I was not able
to get rid of until the war ended six weeks later.

Our truck convoy moved through Pirmasens in starts and
stops. Once we made a long detour through the side streets to
cross a canal on one of the few bridges left standing. During one
long stop we saw a large flight of P-47 Thunderbolts heading
east, with bombs slung under their bellies. Shortly thereafter we
heard a series of heavy explosions in the near distance. During
another long stop we got out of the trucks to stretch, empty our
bladders, and eat a lunch of cold C rations while our noncoms
were called to the head of the convoy for a conference.

When the noncoms returned, Rohan told us that our regiment, which had been in division reserve for two days, was to pass through the 14th Infantry that afternoon and move by truck another twenty-five miles east, to the city of Landau, where we would dig in for the night. Riding trucks again, rather than walking, sounded good to me. But then came the bad news. The 5th Infantry Regiment would attack the next morning, straight east to the Rhine River.

Rohan and I were always interested in maps and where we fit in the big picture, and now he told me that for the coming attack, the 71st Infantry Division—until now part of the XV Corps in the center of the Seventh Army—would be attached to the XX Corps on the army's left flank. From a map I had cut out of the latest issue of *Stars and Stripes*, I could see that this change would put us alongside Patton's now-famous Third Army. Ever since the 1943 campaigns in North Africa and Sicily, Gen. George S. Patton Jr. had been making the headlines, and I had wanted to be able to write home that we were part of his army instead of in the Seventh.

It was midafternoon before our truck convoy finally moved east on the highway out of Pirmasens. The road was straight and lined with trees on either side as far as the eye could see, and there were clouds of black smoke rising ahead. Less than half a mile out of town we came upon the devastation wrought by the P-47s we had seen. First an injured horse approached us, looking bewildered, and then we slowed to a crawl as we moved toward the source of the smoke.

I have never forgotten that sight: The P-47s had utterly wiped out a long column of German horse-drawn artillery, supply wagons, tracked and wheeled vehicles towing antiaircraft guns, and a few Panther tanks. It was the worst carnage I was to see during my time in combat.

There was barely enough room for our trucks to get through what must have been an entire regiment. Some of the horses were still alive in their traces, their entrails spilling out and their legs

kicking feebly as they tried to get up. Then we began to see the
bodies of German soldiers, some so bloody and mangled that it
was hard to recognize them as former living human beings. The
horses and dead Germans were intermingled with smashed howitzers, overturned wagons, boxes, crates, spilled artillery ammunition, rifles, machine pistols, blanket rolls, and packs. Then
came two smashed 88mm guns, more overturned wagons, several
German Volkswagen jeeps with their tires burned off, and at the
head of the column were three Panther tanks with the charred
bodies of crewmen hanging grotesquely from the turrets.

We were all too shocked and nauseated to say much. Not
until we had left the carnage behind did we find our voices, and

CARNAGE EAST OF PIRMASENS

most of our comments were expressions of pity for the dozens of poor horses that were still alive. Someone said we should have stopped to put the wounded animals out of their misery. I silently agreed, but I was not sure I would have had the stomach to participate.

After passing the wreckage, the highway was clear all the way to Landau. The entire 2d Battalion, 5th Infantry, must have been in our convoy, as when we unloaded in the town square I remember counting more than thirty trucks, each carrying twenty to twenty-five infantrymen. I recognized our heavyset battalion commander, Lt. Col. Charles Gettys, waiting by his jeep with Maj. Irving Heymont, the battalion executive officer.

While Captain Neal and the other company commanders gathered around Gettys to receive orders, the rest of us sat on our packs and watched the empty trucks drive around the square and head back out of town to the west.

A few minutes later we moved out on foot, and that afternoon we hiked several miles to a field northeast of Landau, where we dug in for the night. Before dark we learned that our orders for the next day were to attack a town called Germersheim and seize a bridge over the Rhine River. Having just read in *Stars and Stripes* about the miraculous capture of the Remagen bridge, I had a horrible nightmare that night. I dreamed that I was running across the bridge at Germersheim when it blew up. I fell into the river and was drowned.

CHAPTER 15

THE BATTLE FOR GERMERSHEIM AND LINGENFELD

Sunday, March 25, 1945

At dawn we woke to the sound of engines and clanking tank treads on the road bordering the field in which we had dug in for the night. A thin fog lay over the field, but we could see a column of Sherman medium tanks on the road, each with five or six infantrymen clinging to its sloping steel deck behind the turret.

We had been told that our regiment's 3d Battalion was to lead the assault to the Rhine. I wondered if Bill Lueck—my friend and former ASTP roommate who was in K Company of that battalion—was one of the GIs riding atop the tanks.

Word was passed that G Company was to move out in half an hour, which gave us just enough time to heat up our coffee and C rations over a small fire Rohan and I built, using twigs and brush gathered from a nearby woods. When the call came to fall in on the road by platoons, with our mortar section and the supply sergeant's jeep and trailer bringing up the rear, TSgt. Alfred Feltman told us to load our mortars and ammunition vests in the trailer. He explained that we had a long road march ahead and could retrieve the mortars when we deployed for the attack. To be rid of the heavy mortar during the march was welcome news, but the thought of the attack was not.

The mortar section started out in relatively good spirits that morning. The sun had come out, but the air was cool, and we were happy to be rid of the mortars and ammunition we had loaded onto the trailer. The road was bounded on both sides by rolling hills, and after a march of about an hour it curved to the right and began to climb a gentle grade toward a wide cut in the hills ahead.

As we approached the cut, a three-round salvo of long-range German artillery struck the hillside to the left. No one in the column was hit, but word was passed again to be sure to keep our five-yard intervals and not bunch up. After a while, when no further artillery salvos came in, we began to relax. East of the cut the road descended along the shoulder of a long hill overlooking a green plain, with a distant line of trees marking what we assumed was the Rhine River. The river itself was not visible, but we saw houses and a church steeple, and off to the right we could make out another small town.

Halfway down the hill the column stopped and we were ordered to get the mortars and ammo off of the jeep's trailer. We had arrived at the line of departure for the attack.

Minutes later, as we sat on that sun-drenched hillside, waiting for the order to move down the hill, a snarling roar of airplane engines came from behind us, and we looked up to see a full squadron of P-47 Thunderbolts circling overhead. Recalling the captured, German-piloted P-47 that had dropped a bomb near our battalion headquarters outside Lemberg eleven days earlier, we strained our eyes and were relieved to see the American markings on the fighter-bombers.

Suddenly the lead P-47 peeled off, rolled into a steep dive toward the distant town to our left front, and dropped a bomb near its church steeple. We let out a cheer, and for the next several minutes we were treated to the awesome sight of a dozen or so P-47s blasting the town, the name of which we later learned was Lingenfeld.

After the last plane had dropped its bomb the squadron re-formed, circled overhead, and made a series of shallow strafing runs with a rattle of .50-caliber machine guns, then flew off to the west, leaving Lingenfeld covered with smoke. With that came the dreaded order "George Company, move out!"

WATCHING OUR P-47s BOMB LINGENFELD

We advanced down the hill, deployed for the attack in an echelon formation. Leading the way on the left was a rifle platoon and one of our two machine-gun squads. In the center, slightly to the right rear of the lead platoon, came the company's other two rifle platoons. Next in line, just ahead of us, went Captain Neal with his company headquarters group and our second machine-gun squad. And our mortar section of three squads—fifteen men, led by SSgt. Morton Cree—brought up the right rear.

When we reached level ground at the bottom of the hill we saw railroad tracks ahead and a few boxcars on sidings. Parked on our side of the tracks were three odd-looking Sherman tanks with racks of rockets mounted behind their turrets. The rockets fired with a quick series of screeches, one after the other, each trailing orange flames. Once again Lingenfeld—now less than a mile ahead, to our left—was covered with smoke as the rockets hit. When our mortar section passed the three tanks, a crewman wished us luck and said something like "Ya won't have no problem takin' that town now."

A rifle platoon had crossed the tracks to our left and was advancing through a stand of trees toward the nearest houses when the battle began with the *brrrrrrp-brrrrrrp-brrrp* of a German machine gun. This fearsome ripping sound was followed by the snapping of rifle fire from the houses. We rushed for the safety of the railroad embankment just ahead, and as we lay there we saw several riflemen fall as others took cover behind the trees and began to return fire with their M1 rifles.

On our left, huddled behind the end of a boxcar, I recognized our tall company commander, Captain Neal, with part of his headquarters group. During a lull in the firing we heard the cry "*Medic!*," and a medic with Neal's group took off in the direction of the trees, crouching low as he ran. Before he had gone twenty yards he was hit in the head, and his helmet with its red cross painted in a white circle came off as he fell.

"Oh, them dirty Krauts!" someone raged. "Oh, those *bastards*! First they sucker us in with them white flags, and now they're shootin' our medics!"

Sporadic rifle fire continued to come from somewhere, and we ducked when a few rounds went *pssst-pssst* past our ears. From time to time Johnny Rohan and Morton Cree raised their heads to scan the trees and houses with their binoculars. Rohan suggested that we set up the mortars and open fire. But Cree said he had better go check with Captain Neal first; then he backed down the embankment and ran in a crouch over to where the captain and his group were hunkered down by the boxcar, looking at a map.

I recognized two other officers in the group now—one of them the young artillery lieutenant who was our artillery FO, and the other a lieutenant named Silverman, leader of one of our three rifle platoons. Neal looked up in our direction as Cree pointed, and shook his head. Then he and the two lieutenants and Cree bent over the map.

When Cree came running back to where we lay, he said Neal didn't want to chance firing the mortars at such short range, because the lead platoon's radio had apparently been knocked out and there was no way to tell how close the riflemen were to the houses. Then he explained that Silverman's platoon was to move behind us and advance across a plowed field to our right front, in an attempt to outflank the town. Their objective was a line of shrubbery and what looked like a stream at the far end of the field. Our orders were for one mortar squad to follow them while our other two squads set up their tubes where we were, in case the assaulting troops called for mortar fire.

To my dismay, Rohan immediately volunteered our squad to follow the rifle platoon across the plowed field. A wave of fear swept over me when Cree approved. I wanted to curse Rohan and Cree to their faces and demand that, in fairness, the three squad leaders draw straws or flip coins, as they had done that day two weeks earlier when Rohan and I were chosen to ride up to the front in a jeep. But I said nothing; I didn't want the others in the mortar section to see how truly scared I was.

While the other two squads set up their tubes behind us, we

saw Silverman and his riflemen coming our way along the line of boxcars to our left, each man bending low as he dashed across the exposed gaps between the cars. One rifle squad of a dozen men flopped down along the railroad embankment, and its sergeant came over to explain that they were to provide covering fire for the rest of the platoon until the two leading squads were halfway across the field. They would then join the attack, with our single mortar squad bringing up the rear.

Meanwhile, Silverman led his two squads behind us and had them spread out along the embankment to our right. When all was ready, we saw him give the signal. The squad on our left opened fire, and the line of riflemen on our right stood up and advanced across the tracks. I said a prayer as I watched them go, but none fell that I could see. Then we heard the sergeant on our left shout, "Cease fire and follow me!"

Six or seven riflemen sprang to their feet and joined him as he headed across the plowed field in front of us, but the others hesitated, then rose reluctantly when a corporal—their assistant squad leader—cursed them, saying, "C'mon, goddamn it! You heard him!"

Now it was our turn, and Rohan said, "Let's go, guys." I felt my heart pounding as I stood up and slung the strap of the mortar tube over my shoulder.

As I followed Johnny Rohan across the tracks and down the embankment, I looked back just once to make sure that Glen Decker, Waitus Hatley, and Roland Vincent were following me with the mortar base plate and our ammunition. We hadn't gone more than fifty yards when we saw a man in the rifle squad ahead of us fall; then we heard *pffft-pffft* and could see puffs of dirt as slugs burrowed into the furrows at our feet. It was then that I saw bright flashes of a machine gun firing at us from the shrubbery at the far end of the field, and more flashes coming from a grove of trees to our left front. "Oh, sweet Jesus," I heard Decker gasp, "they got us in a crossfire!"

Ignoring the little puffs of dirt from the bullets that seemed to be chasing him, Rohan ran over and knelt down in a furrow by the wounded rifleman. Then he looked back toward the railroad embankment and shouted, "Medic!" Meanwhile, two riflemen just ahead of us ran toward a low mound of freshly dug dirt and suddenly seemed to disappear. Then one raised his head, waved us on, and shouted, "There's a hole here big enough for all of us!" Burdened as we were, the best Decker, Hatley, Vincent, and I could do was break into a clumsy trot toward the safety of that hole.

Hatley and Vincent made it first, and when Decker and I reached the edge of the pit, we dropped our heavy loads and dove in headfirst. My helmet fell off, and as I put out an arm to break my fall, Hatley scrambled out of the way and said, *"Watch out for that pile of crap in the corner!"* But his warning was too late. My outstretched hand came down on a soft pile of human shit, and oh, how I swore! With my other hand I managed to pull a green army-issue handkerchief from my pants pocket, spat on the handkerchief several times, wiped the smelly brown stain from my fingers, and threw the balled-up handkerchief out of the pit.

Shortly after that, Rohan joined us, and now there were seven of us in the hole. When Rohan got his breath, I asked him if the rifleman who got hit was hurt badly, and with a faraway look in his eyes, he nodded his head and his voice cracked as he said, "Neck wound—he bled to death—medic never did come. There was nothin' I could do."

We stayed in that hole for several minutes while Rohan scanned the distant shrubbery with his binoculars. Then he turned to the two riflemen with us and said he could see their squad leader in the bushes ahead, gesturing for us to come on.

"Fuck him," one of them exclaimed. "I ain't leavin' this hole!"

I silently agreed with the scared rifleman, but the other man began to curse, saying, "You chickenshit bastard, c'mon! They *need* us up there!" Then he turned to Rohan and asked, "You an' yer guys comin', Sarge?"

"Sure, Mac," our squad leader replied. "Can't see well enough to fire our mortar from here, but if we can set up in those bushes, maybe we can be of some help. Let's go!" And so the seven of us climbed out of the pit, shouldered our loads, and once again advanced clumsily across the field toward the shrubbery, while Johnny Rohan led the way at a slow trot.

Almost immediately we heard the *brrrrrrp* of a German machine gun firing from the trees to our left, and the rifleman who had wanted to stay behind cried out, "I'm hit!" He fell to his knees, holding his arm, and the other rifleman ran back to him, took a quick look at the wound, and called to Rohan, saying, "Looks like a flesh wound, Sarge, but I better help him back to that hole and put a bandage on it."

The two riflemen ran to the rear in a crouch, leaving our five-man mortar squad on its own. As we trotted on across the freshly plowed field, I could see where the furrows ended and the field stretched flat for another hundred yards or so, to the line of shrubbery in which a few helmets of the riflemen ahead of us were visible. Through gaps in the bushes I could see a silvery patch of water that looked like a pond, and beyond that was a row of trees. From the winking flashes I knew that some of the Krauts were dug in along that line of trees.

Just as we came to the last furrow, another machine gun opened up from our right front, and we could see more flashes coming from a town nestled in another grove of trees. This town, we learned, was Germersheim. We immediately flung ourselves prone in the furrow as tracers flew overhead. For the next minute or so, every time Rohan or I raised up to look, a few bullets hit the little dirt ridge behind which we lay. Luckily none of us was hit, and when the machine gun continued to fire in short bursts, Rohan finally said, "We'll never make it to those bushes. Let's dig in here and get set up to fire."

PINNED DOWN BY ENEMY SMALL ARMS FIRE

Digging in without getting hit in the process was easier said than done. I placed the mortar tube with its folded bipod legs on the ridge of dirt above my head to provide a few extra inches of protection, then I somehow managed to get my pack off. Next, I rolled on my side, unstrapped my little entrenching shovel, and began to scoop dirt and pile it next to the mortar tube—but every time I did so, a bullet either struck the dirt or ricocheted off of the shovel with a *zeeeowww*. I had only managed to deepen the furrow next to where I lay by a few inches when I began to strike rocks. The others were having the same trouble, and after ten minutes or so none of us had dug a hole anywhere deep enough to sit up in, much less erect the mortar tube.

Frustrated, I decided to dig laterally into the softer ridge of dirt on which the mortar lay. When I reached up with my left hand and grasped the folded legs under the tube to move it, I felt a painful blow on a finger and heard a bullet ricochet off into the distance. Certain I had been hit, I pulled my hand out and saw that the stone of the garnet ring I wore was cracked, the gold band was broken at the bottom, and my ring finger was oozing blood from a cut where the band had bitten into it.

When I managed to pull the broken ring off and put it into my shirt pocket, I saw that the bleeding cut was minor, but I regretted losing the ring, which my parents had given me on my eighteenth birthday. I was never sure whether the garnet stone had been hit directly, or was smashed by the impact of a ricochet off the tube. Whatever the case, I was lucky. That little cut on my finger was the first of two minor "scratches" I suffered during my time in combat.

The sun was hot as we lay there in the shallow furrow, and before long most of us had consumed all of the tepid water in our canteens. The firing had died down when we stopped digging, and Rohan raised his head cautiously to scan the shrubbery to our front and the village of Germersheim in the trees to our right. I looked up and recognized Lieutenant Silverman running left along the line of bushes, followed by a squad of riflemen. I saw him turn and pump his raised fist in the standard infantry signal meaning "Follow me, double time," and two or three men followed him down the slope toward a finger of water I took to be part of the pond.

There was a sudden burst of machine-gun fire from across the pond, and we ducked. When we raised our heads again there was no sign of Silverman or the men who had followed him, but we heard a shout, *"Pull back, pull back!"* coming from a grove of trees on our left, overlooking the slope and the pond. Shortly we saw several riflemen rise from the bushes to our front, zigzag up the slope, and disappear into the safety of the grove, with bullets kicking up puffs of dirt around their heels. Miraculously, no one was hit that I could see, but for the next several minutes we could hear what sounded like sniper fire coming from across the pond, and every so often a bullet smacked the dirt above the furrow where we lay. We were pinned down and couldn't fire our mortar. I began to wonder if we would ever get out of the fix we were in. I thought, *Where in hell is our artillery?*

A minute later, as if in answer to my question, we heard a high-velocity *whoosh* overhead, and then a single shell exploded with a loud *crrrack* in the bushes to our front, throwing up a huge fountain of clods and uprooted shrubs. When some of the clods fell near where we lay, Rohan observed, "Jeezus, that was no 105 howitzer. They don't make *that* kinda sound. Must have been a 155 Long Tom. Look how high it blew those bushes!"

A long minute passed, then a salvo of four large-caliber shells *whooshed* in. Three exploded somewhere across the pond, and the last shell struck the slope at the edge of the grove of trees to our left. This time we heard the *whiz* of shrapnel, and then we heard a voice from the grove crying for a medic.

"Shit!" Rohan exclaimed. "That last one was short and got one of our own guys! Keep your heads down in case there are more coming!"

When minutes had passed and no more of our shells came in, we raised our heads and saw two men emerge from the grove and run across the plowed field toward our position. Leading the way was our platoon runner, Corporal Zarimba, who was carrying his rifle and a walkie-talkie. Behind him came Pvt. Shaky Hayes, one of Bailey's ammunition bearers, who was wearing a vest full of mortar shells. They flopped down in the furrow next to us, and Zarimba gasped that Feltman—our platoon sergeant—had been hit by a piece of shrapnel. He added that Cree had taken over the platoon, Rohan was to take over as mortar section leader, and now Captain Neal wanted all the mortar fire he could get on the Krauts dug in across the pond. Knowing that we had only a total of twelve mortar shells with us, Cree had sent Hayes to us with his six extra shells.

Rohan explained that the rocks prevented us from digging holes deep enough to set up our tube, and that in any case the far side of the pond looked to be closer than the minimum range of our mortar. Then he asked why the two mortar squads back at the railroad didn't do the job, as they had a walkie-talkie by which their fire could be adjusted. Zarimba explained that Hayes had been sent up to report that their radio battery was dead, so Neal and Cree had decided it was up to us. With that, Rohan told Zarimba to get Cree on his walkie-talkie.

The upshot of all this was that I was told to take over the squad and continue to try to dig a hole deep enough to set up the mortar. Rohan ran over to the grove of trees to get a better fix on where Captain Neal wanted us to fire. He would relay the word back to us, by radio. We watched Rohan run in a crouch, and I held my breath until he had disappeared safely into the trees. Then Decker and I began to dig again.

We were still digging but had many inches yet to go when Zarimba's radio squawked and Rohan's voice told us to forget about firing the mortar; Captain Neal had called for a platoon of tanks to move up through our position and engage the Krauts across the pond. So the six of us—Zarimba, Hayes, Decker, Hatley, Vincent, and myself—lay there in the sun, waiting for the tanks to come. Zarimba had taken over Rohan's shallow slit trench to my left, Hayes was to his left, and the others were to my right. Exhausted from digging, I closed my eyes and dozed off until I heard engines and the clanking of tank tracks behind us. I turned to see three tanks lumbering across the plowed field toward our position.

In the lead was a Sherman M4 medium tank, flanked on either side by a light tank. All three were buttoned up, and I began to wonder if they could see us, so I raised up and waved at them frantically. With that they lurched to a halt, a turret hatch on the

Sherman opened, and one of its crewmen jumped down and ran forward in a crouch. He had a submachine gun cradled in his arms. At his direction, the three tanks swung slightly left and followed him slowly across the field a few yards beyond where Hayes lay. Then the crewman climbed back up into the tank's turret and closed the hatch with a *clang*.

In line-abreast formation, the three tanks advanced slowly toward the shrubs on this side of the pond. When I could no longer see them without exposing myself by raising up on my elbows, I ducked down and waited, expecting any minute to hear them open fire with their cannons and machine guns.

Suddenly, a nearby concussion seemed to suck the air from my lungs, and I felt as if something had lifted me bodily and hit me in the pit of the stomach. With my ears ringing and the acrid stink of high explosive in my nostrils, I looked over at Zarimba and gasped, "What the *hell* was that?"

He looked at me wide-eyed, shook his head, and when we raised up to look at the tanks, we saw a smoking gash in the hard ground not more than a yard in front of our furrow. Seconds later we heard a *whump* and saw smoke rising from the Sherman tank. It was then that I guessed that the Krauts had fired two *Panzerfaust* antitank rockets; the first one had missed its intended target and nearly got Zarimba and me.

The Sherman's turret hatches flew open and we saw four men climb out, jump to the ground, and come running back toward us. One of them dragged a leg as two others helped him. Meanwhile, the two light tanks had pivoted and also were coming back, raising clouds of dust as they followed the four running men. The man in the lead flung himself down into the furrow next to Hayes and gasped, "Fuckin' goddamn *Panzerfaust* killed our driver!" When his three companions and the two light tanks reached our position, one of the tanks stopped just long enough for the four crewmen to climb aboard its rear deck; then it followed the other light tank back toward the safety of the railroad embankment as a few shots from somewhere hurried them on their way.

So much for tanks, I thought, disgusted that not *one* of them had fired a single shot during the entire affair. I was swept by a terrible urge to get up and run for the rear. Here we were—six men in all—pinned down in an open field by snipers dug in to our front and in the village of Germersheim to our right. Even if we had managed to dig a deep enough pit for our one mortar, I knew we were too close for the mortar to fire if the Krauts counterattacked. In that event, all we had with which to defend ourselves were Zarimba's M1 rifle; the carbines carried by Hayes, Hatley, and Vincent; the .45-caliber pistols with which Decker and I were armed; and a few hand grenades.

Although Rohan had left me in charge of the squad, Zarimba outranked me by one stripe, so I turned to him and asked, "What should we do now? Stay here or try to make a run for it back to the railroad or over to those trees on our left?"

"I dunno," he replied. "Maybe by now Bailey's got a radio that works an' the two mortars back there can give us some covering fire. Lemme call Cree or the Old Man and find out."

He spoke softly into his walkie-talkie, then listened for a long minute and finally said, "Yes, sir, Captain. Roger and out." Then he turned to me and said, "The Old Man says for us to sit tight. Battalion is sendin' Fox Company and some more tanks to clear out the snipers from that town on the right, and they'll try to outflank the Krauts on the other side of the pond."

So the six of us lay in the hot sun and waited, and waited, and Hayes complained of thirst and asked if any of us had any water left, but we were all thirsty and had long since drained our canteens dry. Minutes passed, then over on our right a tank gun barked, machine guns chattered, and we could see three Sherman tanks advancing on the nearest houses nestled in the trees. A squad of infantry followed close behind the tanks. I held my breath, half expecting to see one or more of the tanks get hit by a *Panzerfaust*, but they disappeared into the trees, machine guns blazing away, and suddenly we saw a white flag waving from one of the houses. The firing stopped.

After a minute another tank gun fired from somewhere in the village. I watched the shells explode in the trees on the far side of the pond. As I watched, I said over and over to myself, "*Kill the bastards! Kill all the goddamn bastards!*" I figured that would be the end of the battle.

When the tanks in Germersheim ceased firing, Hayes crawled over and offered to take all of our canteens back to fill them with water from a pit in which the battalion aid station was located. He had passed the pit on his way up to report to Cree, and the medics had let him fill his canteen from a five-gallon jerry can of water. In hindsight, Zarimba and I should not have allowed Hayes to go on this errand, but as the firing had stopped and we were all tired and thirsty, we agreed.

Hayes left his carbine and mortar ammunition vest with us, gathered up all of our aluminum canteens, hooked his fingers through the cap chains, stood up, and started trotting slowly back across the plowed field in the direction of the railroad embankment. Watching him go, and seeing how the sun reflected from the shiny canteens, I thought, *Oh, my God, he's a perfect target if there are any Kraut snipers still alive.*

And sure enough, Hayes had not gone more than fifty yards when telltale puffs of dirt rose around his boots. Then he sat down suddenly and turned to look at us. I could see that he was holding his leg.

"Oh, Christ, he's hit!" someone exclaimed.

"Shaky," I shouted, "are you hit?" He nodded. "Then get *down*!" I shouted. I looked at Zarimba and said, "Someone's gotta go help him." I suppose I was hoping someone would volunteer, but Zarimba and the others looked at me as if to say, "Why don't *you* go?"

I hesitated, thinking that if Rohan were here he'd go in a

minute. So I said, "Okay then, I'll go," and without another word I took off in a running crouch. With the adrenaline pumping, I must have covered those fifty yards in ten or fifteen seconds, and flopped down in the furrow next to Shaky.

"Where ya hit?" I gasped, and he pulled up his pant leg to show me a slightly bleeding gash on his shin.

"Not so bad, Shakey," I said. "Christ, you were lucky. Listen, you can't run very fast with that, so you better stay here and keep the hell down until I can get a medic to come up. Lemme have those canteens, and I'll see if I can get the water while I'm at it. Just point me out where that aid station is."

He raised up on an elbow and pointed to a dirt mound halfway to the railroad embankment. I recognized it as the pit in which I had fallen into the pile of German crap earlier that morning. Looking at the shiny canteens gave me an idea. I quickly took off my pistol belt, removed my field jacket and spread it out in the furrow, buckled the pistol back on, piled the canteens on the jacket, rolled it into a bundle, and tied the arms in a knot.

"Okay, here I go," I said. I cradled the bundle in my arms, took a deep breath, jumped up, and began to zigzag across the plowed field toward the mound of dirt. This time I was careful to slide feet-first into the pit in which three medics sat by their satchels, smoking cigarettes. I set my bundle of canteens down and one of them said, "Hey, Mac, we seen ya comin'. Ya hit?"

I shook my head, and when I had caught my breath I said, "I'm okay, but we got one guy with a leg wound out there in the field where I came from. And I think there're more wounded over in some trees where George Company's CP is. They need your help up there."

One of the medics, who wore the stripes of a T5 corporal, shook his head and said, "Sorry, bud, battalion surgeon won't let any more of us go up until you guys clean out them snipers. Two of our guys got killed already—shot right in the head. Damn Krauts are usin' the red crosses on our helmets as bull's-eyes!"

I glared at him and said that Fox Company was attacking and by now probably had killed or captured all of the snipers.

"Don't shit *me,* Mac," the T5 said. "We was watchin' ya runnin' toward us just now, and I seen at least a dozen slugs kick up dirt right by yer heels. Yer damn lucky to be alive!"

Acting the tough infantryman, trying not to show how this shook me up, I said I had no choice but to head back and risk it, as those were my buddies out there who needed help. Then I looked at the jerry cans of water in the pit and said that the least they could do was to let me fill the canteens I had brought.

The medics agreed readily and helped me fill the canteens. Then came my moment of truth. I wanted in the worst way to stay in the safety of that pit! So I procrastinated, took a long swig of water, and refilled my canteen. It was several minutes before I mustered the courage to climb out and head back across the plowed field with my heavy bundle.

Waiting those extra few minutes may have saved me from being George Company's last casualty on that bloody Palm Sunday. Just after I flopped down again in the furrow next to Shaky Hayes and gave him his full canteen, we saw Fox Company's riflemen emerge from the town of Germersheim on our right. As they approached the trees on the far side of the pond, several helmeted Krauts jumped up, waving white flags. With their surrender, G Company's part in the battle for Germersheim and Lingenfeld ended.

It was late afternoon before a medic finally arrived, bandaged Shaky's leg, and sent him limping back to the rear while the rest of us moved over to the grove of trees on our left. There we joined Johnny Rohan and dug in for the night behind a machine-gun position overlooking the slope and the pond.

We could see two bodies sprawled face up at the foot of the

slope, one of them half in the water. Rohan told us they were Lieutenant Silverman and his platoon runner. Then he turned, and pointed at a dark form covered with a raincoat in the trees behind us. Grief and anger were in his voice when he said, "That's Feltman over there. He took a piece of shrapnel in his arm when the 155s came in short, but he wasn't hurt bad. He'd still be alive if that damn nervous Nellie Lieutenant Tyler hadn't *ordered* him to go back to the rear for first aid. And when he stood up to go, a sniper got him right in the back of the head!"

It wasn't until the next morning that we learned the full story of the battle. Eleven George Company men were killed that day, and someone told me there were 20 wounded. In one day, out of a full-strength total of 186 men, our company had suffered more than 16 percent casualties.

Several G Company soldiers earned medals for heroism in that battle. But it was not until after the war ended that I learned who they all were and what they had done. The most notable of these was a tall rifle squad leader, SSgt. William Randall, who climbed a wall around a house on the outskirts of Germersheim and shot several scurrying Germans who were trying to get their vehicles in the courtyard started. Randall then led his men in the capture of the house and held the place all night long against several German attempts to recapture it. He received the Silver Star in a ceremony a few weeks later.

CHAPTER 16

POSTMORTEM ON THE RHINE, AND TRANSFER TO PATTON'S THIRD ARMY

Monday, March 26, through Saturday, March 31, 1945

The temperature fell to below freezing during the night after the battle for Germersheim and Lingenfeld ended; it was the most miserable night I ever spent in a foxhole. We had long since left our heavy overcoats and extra blankets in our duffel bags, somewhere to the rear on regimental supply trucks, and our thin sleeping bags and raincoats were not enough to keep us warm. Several times during that long night I awoke shivering with cold and climbed out of my hole to urinate on a tree, stamp my feet, and blow clouds of steam.

Dawn came at last, and someone passed the welcome word that when the sun rose we could build a fire to heat water for coffee. As Decker, Hatley, Vincent, and I squatted by our fire, drinking C ration instant coffee and heating up our breakfast cans of hash or ham and eggs, Rohan came over with two M1 rifles and an extra rifleman's cartridge belt, complete with bayonet, on his shoulder. With him was the surly southern kid Packard.

Rohan ceremoniously handed me one of the rifles and the extra cartridge belt and explained that as I was the new squad leader, Glen Decker would take over as gunner, with Waitus Hatley as his assistant. Roland Vincent would now be the number one ammo bearer, and Packard would join us as the number two ammo bearer. From the sour look on Packard's face I could see that he was not too happy, and I soon learned that he resented taking orders from me.

Now that I had the coveted M1, Hatley inherited my pistol and belt, and Rohan told him to turn his carbine in to the supply sergeant who had come up with his jeep and trailer to collect the weapons of those who had been killed or wounded. Staff Sergeant Cree, who had taken over Feltman's job as weapons platoon sergeant, joined us, and for the next half hour or so we sat around our little fire, each of us telling stories of the battle as we had seen it.

Rohan retold the story of how Feltman still would be alive if Lieutenant Tyler hadn't ordered him to go back to the aid station to have his arm wound treated. Cree told how he had seen my friend Pvt. Jesus Lozano, an assistant machine gunner, heroically take over the weapon when the gunner was wounded, and fire belt after belt before he was shot through the head and killed. We also learned that our quiet young executive officer, First Lieutenant Doneski, had been badly wounded. And Rohan said that Lieutenant Silverman apparently had thought that the pond was just a small creek when he tried to lead his men in a charge toward the Kraut positions. When he was hit and killed, his runner ran out into the deep water to try to retrieve his body but also was killed. As the stories and casualty count went on and on, the magnitude of George Company's near-disastrous losses began to sink in.

While we sat there talking, we saw eight men trudge up the slope from the edge of the pond, carrying two poncho-wrapped bodies we knew were those of Silverman and his runner. We fell silent until they had trudged past us up into the trees. Then Cree said that for several hours after they were killed, snipers had continued to use their dead bodies for target practice. Rohan added that two of George Company's five medics had been shot through the head, confirming what I had been told the previous afternoon by the battalion medics in the aid station pit.

These stories so enraged me that I readily agreed with someone who swore, "*By God, from now on we take no prisoners!*" I thank God that no one in my squad actually kept to that vow during the many battles to come.

Shortly after Cree and Rohan left, three riflemen came over to our fire and asked for a volunteer to help them bring in a body that had been left overnight by an irrigation ditch leading from the pond toward a distant house on our left. I saw Packard shoot me a challenging look, then avert his eyes when I glared back at him. I knew it was up to me to set an example, so I handed my new rifle to Decker and stood up.

"I'll go," I said. "Lead the way."

We walked down the slope toward the irrigation ditch, followed it for about a hundred yards, and there lay the body in the weeds, chin thrown back, eyes and mouth open, arms outstretched stiffly, rifle and helmet nearby. I forced myself to look at the man's swollen tongue, contorted black-and-blue face, and the ugly hole above one bloodshot eye. I saw how the rivulets of blood had run down his cheek and soaked the collar of his field jacket.

As I watched, someone fumbled for his dog tags, looked at one of them briefly, and said, "Yeah, this one is Quinn, all right." Another GI placed the dead man's helmet over his face and fastened the chin strap around the back of his bloody head, saying, "No one wants to look at that."

We had no stretcher, but we had brought a blanket. Somehow the four of us carried the stiff body back along the irrigation ditch and up into the trees to a fence, where we carefully lowered it to the ground alongside several other covered corpses.

VOLUNTEERS BRING IN PRIVATE QUINN'S BODY

Well, I thought, *I've done my share.* Before I turned away I wanted to say something like, "Quinn, I didn't know you, but may you rest in peace." I remembered one of war correspondent Ernie Pyle's poignant columns in a newspaper I had read back in Benning. In that famous column Pyle told about a beloved captain whose body had been brought down an Italian mountain on a mule, and how several of his men had come over to look into his dead face and tell him how sorry they were. I had to stifle an urge to look for Feltman's body among the corpses by the fence, under the trees, and tell him the same thing.

When I finally headed back to join my squad, I heard loud, angry voices as I came out of the trees, and I saw several riflemen in a circle around a frightened German prisoner who held a leaflet in his hand. One of the riflemen had a bayonet on his rifle and held it against the prisoner's chest, while another shouted questions at him in German.

When the German tried to hand his interrogator the leaflet—an invitation to surrender and be treated according to the Geneva Convention rules of warfare—the man with the bayonet said, "Tell the bastard that fuckin' piece of paper don't mean shit to me! We're gonna shoot him anyway!" As I joined the angry group, someone else said, "Ask him who shot our medics!" Another rifleman kicked the pleading prisoner viciously in the rump.

I had never been this close to a live prisoner, who smelled as if he had crapped in his pants, and I remember wanting to vent

CLOSE CONTACT WITH A FRIGHTENED GERMAN POW

my fury by adding a kick of my own. But just then the riflemen's platoon leader shouldered his way past me, reminded his men it was against all the rules to mistreat prisoners, and ordered two of them to march the poor German back to battalion headquarters for interrogation. With that the others dispersed and I walked off to join my mortar squad.

At about noon that day our regimental commander, Col. Sidney C. Wooten, and our battalion commander, Lt. Col. Charles Gettys, joined Captain Neal in a clearing not far from our position. From the way Wooten put his hand on Neal's shoulder I guessed he was trying to console him over the terrible losses our company had suffered. The three officers spent some time looking at a map, and not long after Wooten and Gettys had left, we received orders to pack up and get ready to move out.

Although the 5th Infantry Regiment had taken hundreds of prisoners after the battle, many more hundreds had escaped over the river before the Germersheim bridge was blown. We were told that our 71st Division was going to be transferred into the Third Army, whose leading divisions had crossed the Rhine. How excited we were to learn that we were to join the famous Gen. George Patton, whose engineers were building a pontoon bridge up near Mannheim.

That afternoon, March 26, we moved by truck and jeep on a dusty ride through the town of Neuhofen, and from there to the city of Speyer, on the west bank of the Rhine some fifteen miles north of Germersheim. And so ended our sixteenth day in combat.

During our brief stay in Speyer we had our first close contact with German civilians, most of them women and children. Rumors of spies abounded after a few rounds of German artillery struck a motor pool of American trucks parked in a field not far from the house in which we were billeted. And a woman was said to have been caught in the attic of a house using a flashlight to signal the motor pool's location to German observers on the east side of the Rhine.

Because of this, early on our first morning in Speyer all civilians who lived on the street closest to the river were forced to evacuate. I for one regarded all but the youngest children as Nazis and potential spies, and I turned a deaf ear to several crying women who begged me for permission to stay in their houses.

Another rumor was that several German soldiers who had not been able to escape over the river had been caught wearing American officers' uniforms, so we were warned to challenge anyone we did not recognize. True or not, when a captain I had never seen before suddenly opened the door to the room in the house where we were billeted and asked what outfit we were with, I thought I detected a German accent. I was about to screw up enough courage to ask him for his ID when I noticed the chaplain's insignia on his collar, and someone who obviously knew him said, "Good morning, padre. We're George Company, sir. Fifth Infantry Regiment."

Later that morning I wrote a letter home, and although censorship prohibited the mention of Speyer or the fact that we were now in Patton's Third Army, the rules had been relaxed enough for me to write that the 71st Infantry Division had been part of the Seventh Army and had fought in the Alsation region of France and the Saar region of Germany. The following excerpt from that letter gives some idea of my state of mind after seventeen days of combat and two days after the battle for Germersheim and Lingenfeld.

As for this division, we've seen two engagements to date. The last one is just a day or so old, and here we are miles away already, so it shows the Germans still west of the Rhine are on the run. As you can imagine, this combat business isn't easy to tell about, and is certainly no fun. I've heard lots of guys in such outfits as the Field Artillery and Air Corps say that their work is exciting at times, and often rough. Well, the infantryman's war is certainly never exciting and is without the slightest doubt the dirtiest, roughest job of them all—but of course I know that Ernie Pyle has already long ago convinced you, as he did me. The thing that keeps us going, through it all, is just each other. We're all in it together, and we're all buddies.

Truthfully, I've seen a lot more the past few days—my friends killed and wounded—than I ever thought I could take, or would see, in even a month. Am enclosing the shoulder strap of a whimpering ex-superman—a German 1st Sgt—who was one of our company's large catch of the last engagement.

When not on guard in the street outside our house, most of us spent the time huddled around a modern downdraft stove fueled with charcoal blocks found in the cellar. That afternoon one of Bailey's squad—a Cherokee Indian named Willie Burns—went to the cellar for more charcoal and brought up a full case of champagne he had found hidden under the pile of charcoal blocks. We warned him it might be poisoned, but Burns unhesitatingly popped the cork on a bottle, took a sip, then a long swig. When he pronounced it okay, several others in the room grabbed for a bottle.

Still a professed teetotaler, although I had imbibed a cup of hard cider and had had a taste of Calvados back at Camp Old Gold a few weeks earlier, I watched my buddies guzzle the stuff down like lemonade. Hatley kept insisting on pouring me a canteen cupful from his bottle, and I finally gave in. I drank a cup, then a second, and then a third, in the hope it would help me forget the painful memory of Germersheim.

Sure enough, I was soon laughing and joking with the rest of them, feeling no pain, and saying to myself, *So this is what it feels like to get drunk.* Meanwhile, Willie Burns had gone outside with two bottles after explaining that he was taking them to the men on guard.

Sometime later we heard a woman screaming hysterically in German, and several of us rushed out into the street to see what the trouble was. I knew just enough German to understand that an *"Amerikanische Soldat"* was threatening to shoot everyone in her house, including her children. So she had come down the street screaming for help. The distraught woman led the way as she begged us to hurry. We followed her up the steps and into the open door of a house from which we could hear another woman crying, *"Nein, nein, ach du lieber Gott, bitte nichts shiessen!"* (No, no, oh, my dear God, please don't shoot!) And there on the floor in the entry hall we saw Willie Burns gripping a frightened little boy by the neck and trying to shove the muzzle of his .45 pistol into the boy's mouth.

Willie turned when I shouted, "No, goddamnit, Willie, no!" I could see he was crying. Somehow I wrestled the automatic out of his hand, the three men with me forced him to release the child, pinned his arms behind his back, and hustled him out the door with me in their wake. I kicked away an empty champagne bottle as we came down the steps, and it struck me that the old adage about Indians not being able to drink without going berserk must be true. In any case, here was Willie Burns—a full-blooded Cherokee Indian from Oklahoma—so drunk he practically had to be carried.

On the way he kept repeating, between sobs of grief, that he wanted to kill every German because they had killed his best and only friend, Jesus Lozano. When we got Willie back into our house, someone suggested we tie him up, but all we did was put him to bed in a windowless storage room and lock the door. When we let him out the next morning he was very apologetic for the trouble he had caused, and so hung over he swore he would never touch another drop.

That afternoon—it must have been Wednesday, March 28—we were issued division insignia decals and told to paste them on the right side of our helmet, as by now the Germans knew that the 71st was in the line. The insignia was a slanted blue "*71*" on a circular white background ringed with red. For this reason we were often referred to as "The Red Circle Division."

I had just finished pasting the insignia on my helmet when our first mail in a week was delivered. In addition to several letters, I received a welcome box of cookies and doughnuts. Before I could read the letters or open the box, word came to get ready to move out in ten minutes. We were told to prepare for a "long motor move" to the town of Neustadt, northwest of Speyer, and were warned that German stragglers had ambushed an earlier convoy on the main highway. For this reason, an advance party of jeeps from our battalion's I&R (Intelligence and Reconnaissance) Platoon was to lead the way, detouring around the known enemy-infested area.

At the last minute it was decided that the advance party should take a mortar along, and my squad was assigned the dubious honor of riding on one of the I&R Platoon's overloaded jeeps rather than go with the main truck convoy.

What a wild and scary jeep ride that was! Much of it was cross-country, through dark woods and up narrow trails. I remember hanging on for dear life and worrying that we were lost and might at any moment be killed or captured. Even so, I managed to open my box and pass it around, and the cookies and doughnuts were all gone when we reached the safety of Neustadt just after dark.

In Neustadt it was officially confirmed that we were now in Patton's Third Army. For many of us the flamboyant George Patton's reputation evoked admiration bordering on idolatry, and I looked forward to the time when we would be permitted to write home with this exciting news. It was said that Patton's armored spearheads had crossed the Rhine and were already deep into the

German heartland, and that after we crossed the river we would have little more to do than move fast and mop up. This was not quite true, as it turned out. But there was some truth to the "moving fast" part of it.

With the arrival of a truckload of replacements, George Company was brought back to full strength before we left Neustadt. Shaky Hayes also returned, wearing a bandage on his shin, which he proudly removed to show us how his wound was healing. As for the many other George Company men who had been wounded at *Germersheim*, to my knowledge none ever returned to combat. It is of course possible that some of them died of their wounds.

Just after sundown we were reminded that there was still a war on when a German fighter plane made a low-level strafing run down one of Neustadt's main streets, causing no casualties before it fled back to the east. Someone said this had occurred on each of the two preceding nights since Neustadt had been captured, and for this reason the lone plane was known as "Bed Check Charlie."

We entrucked just before midnight on Thursday, March 29, to begin a long motor drive to the north. All we were told was that we were joining the XII Corps of Patton's army, and would cross the Rhine in the vicinity of the city of Worms.

Driving with blackout lights, our long convoy crept along for several hours, much of the time in low gear. Just before dawn on March 30 the truck ahead of us stopped very suddenly. We rammed into its tailgate, were rammed in turn by the truck behind us, and for the next several seconds we heard a series of metal-on-metal bangs and clangs as the chain reaction progressed back along the length of the convoy. Were it not for the fact that we had been moving so slowly, there might have been serious injuries; but luckily there were none so far as we knew.

Shortly thereafter, while the convoy was still sitting stationary on that narrow road, a jeep roared by with its siren howling, and I got a glimpse of a helmeted figure in the passenger's seat, wearing a row of stars on the shoulder straps of his raincoat.

"Holy Christ!" someone exclaimed. "That's ole Blood an' Guts Patton hisself!" It was not light enough for me to be sure it was he, but many years later I deduced from reading his memoir *War As I Knew It* that he had been in the area on March 30, 1945. In any case, the convoy soon began to move, and that morning when we detrucked at a town called Rockenhausen, the story made the rounds that it had indeed been Patton in the jeep, and that he had gone ahead to straighten out a traffic jam at a crossroads where part of a French armored unit being shifted south to the Seventh Army had blocked the way.

OUR CONVOY OVERTAKEN BY GENERAL PATTON'S JEEP

When the movie *Patton* made its debut sometime in the 1970s, it included an episode just like this one, where Patton served as a traffic cop.

Our stay in Rockenhausen, which was the division's main assembly area for our forthcoming move across the Rhine, lasted a brief twelve hours. The March 30 entry in my pocket diary notebook includes the terse comment: "Last hot meal—spinach—wait for QM [quartermaster] trucks—leave 7 PM."

All I remember of that "hot meal" was that our cooks told us to enjoy it, because Patton had ordered that in the Third Army, unlike the Seventh, the supply priority for units across the river would be fuel and ammunition in that order. His order also said that there would be no more hot meals prepared by company kitchen trucks until the war ended! That story turned out to be true. We never saw our company kitchen truck again.

Although the road distance to the Rhine was only about thirty miles, it was not until 5:00 A.M. on Saturday, March 31, that our convoy finally rumbled across the fabled river on a pontoon bridge near Worms, after ten hours of slow travel. En route we had spent more time stopped than moving, and once we had to wait half an hour while a column of tanks passed. Moving an infantry regiment of nearly four thousand men requires about two hundred trucks, in a convoy at least four miles long. Anyone who knows about gridlock on today's freeways can appreciate how the slightest holdup at the head of a column can cause long delays.

All I can remember of the river crossing itself was the stink of diesel exhaust fumes and a smoke screen so thick we couldn't see more than a hundred yards in any direction. The smoke screen had been laid by artillery to obscure the bridge from German dive bombers, which were said to have made several attempts to knock it out.

Once we were on the autobahn leading north to Darmstadt we made good time, but the highway was bordered on both sides by thick evergreen forests, and I worried about ambushes. This

CROSSING THE RHINE RIVER IN A SMOKE SCREEN

worry stemmed from the rumor that Patton's fast-moving armor had bypassed a full division of SS troops who were making nightly raids on his supply lines in the vicinity of Frankfurt, and it would be our job to clean them out. This rumor gained credibility that afternoon when our battalion was ordered to leave the autobahn and follow a tank company into Neu Isenburg, a suburb just south of Frankfurt.

As the tanks led the way down the main street of the town, a single rifle shot rang out, and the convoy of trucks suddenly halted. Within minutes our entire 2d Battalion was off the trucks to begin a house-to-house search for snipers. We found no snipers, and no more shots were fired, but it took hours to search the hundreds of frightened civilians we lined up in the streets.

MPs arrived, and these civilians—whose houses and apartments we took over for the night—were unceremoniously sent to spend the night elsewhere. Word was passed that a rear guard of SS troops had pulled out of town just ahead of our convoy, and that we would set out after them in the morning.

George Company was billeted that night of March 31, 1945, in a small hotel on the main street of Neu Isenburg. There was no electricity or hot water, but we made do with candles and cold water sponge baths. We were especially happy to sleep on real beds under heavy German comforters.

CHAPTER 17

BUDINGER WALD AND THE 6TH SS MOUNTAIN DIVISION NORD

Sunday, April 1, through Wednesday, April 4, 1945

Easter Sunday, April 1, also was our April Fools' Day. My entry for that day was brief: "1st April, Easter Sunday. Set out after SS troopers, 6th SS Division Nord reported in woods. Hike all day, 25 miles. Good billet, I wash my feet at last."

Just before dawn that morning George Company lined up in front of the hotel in which we had spent the night. As the day's advance was to be a long one, all on foot, we mortarmen thankfully left our mortars and ammunition on the supply sergeant's jeep and trailer, which would follow close behind. Before moving out, we were told that the SS troops who had left Neu Isenburg the previous afternoon were part of the 6th SS Mountain Division Nord—an elite unit only recently arrived in Germany from occupied Norway and Denmark. It was said that many of them could be expected to be so fanatic that they would rather die for *Der Führer* than be captured.

As we marched out of town on either side of the street, keeping five-yard intervals, a bell began to ring from the steeple of a Catholic church we were approaching. This reminded me that it was Easter Sunday.

"First Mass," someone said, and someone else said, "First Mass my ass, there's a curfew until sunrise! I bet that's a signal to let the SS know we're coming!"

We ran into no resistance that day, except for a few inaccurate rifle shots fired at long range, and we spent the night in the city of Hanau, several miles east of Frankfurt.

The next morning—Monday, April 2—word was passed that several hundred SS troops were trapped by our sister regiments—the 14th and the 66th—in a forest northeast of Hanau. To finish them off, our 5th Infantry Regiment was to move by truck to an assembly area from which we would attack head-on into the woods, with our 2d Battalion in the lead. This news was not greeted with much enthusiasm. And there was more bad news to come: George Company was to take the point in the attack, supported by a platoon of tanks, while E, F, and H Companies followed us.

After we had our C ration breakfast, the 2d Battalion loaded up on trucks and moved east out of Hanau a few miles, then left the highway and turned north on a dirt road to a clearing on the edge of a forest. There we offloaded next to a platoon of Sherman tanks. We stood around in that clearing for a long time, waiting for orders, while our officers conferred with Lieutenant Colonel Gettys and the tank platoon leader, who, much to our surprise, was a light-skinned Negro officer—a second lieutenant.

We learned later that the armor attached to our division was the 761st Tank Battalion, an all-Negro outfit about which a book was written after the war. It was the only all-Negro tank battalion in Eisenhower's European armies.

At last came the order to move out. Two of George Company's three rifle platoons were formed into a skirmish line and moved off into the forest on either side of a woodcutter's trail. The rest of the company followed in a column of twos on the trail itself. Like most German forests, the woods through which we moved were free of underbrush; hence our skirmishers made little noise as they advanced. From time to time we could see their squad leaders signal for a halt while scouts went ahead to check out clearings and suspicious-looking stacks of logs. As we marched along the trail, expecting at any moment to hear a German machine gun open up, I thanked God I was not one of the scouts.

By late afternoon we had cleared several large patches of forest but had flushed no SS troops. Several times a few panicked deer had startled us as they fled.

Just before dusk we returned to our starting point, climbed back aboard our trucks, and were driven north to the town of Budingen, where we arrived just before midnight. The entry in my diary for April 2 reads: "No SS troops. Mission snafu, wrong woods, 5 mi hike turns out to be 15 miles."

Our mortar section spent an uncomfortable short night sleeping on benches in an empty butcher shop. At dawn we woke to the sound of tanks and jeeps in the street, and word was passed that today we would see action for sure. We were told that the remnants of the 6th SS Mountain Division Nord were now trapped in a forest known as Budinger Wald, on a high plateau a short distance southeast of Budingen. We bitched and groaned when told that Colonel Wooten, our regimental CO, had once again selected our 2d Battalion to make the attack, while the lucky 1st and 3rd Battalions moved by truck to set up blocking positions east of the woods.

The good news was that this time E and F Companies would lead the attack on foot, followed by an assortment of tanks, jeeps, and three-quarter-ton trucks carrying the battalion headquarters, G Company, and H Company.

By 8:00 A.M. we had finished a quick C ration breakfast, had our coffee, and were lined up in front of the butcher shop, watching the long files of E and F Company riflemen disappear up two steep trails leading to the forested plateau. Following E Company up one of the narrow switchback trails were two jeeps carrying our battalion commander and his staff. Our three mortar squads were assigned to follow Gettys aboard several H Company jeeps. Bringing up the rear was the rest of G Company mounted in jeeps and trucks, and atop a platoon of tanks.

I fell asleep during that slow jeep ride up the mountain, but I awoke with a start just before 9:00 A.M., when the battle began.

The battle for the Budinger Wald began when we heard the first German machine guns open up on E Company as it advanced

TAKING COVER AS THE BUDINGER WALD BATTLE STARTS

through the thick woods, just ahead of us. Our column of jeeps and tanks came to an abrupt halt, and when the sounds of the firefight grew in intensity, the order was passed to dismount. We jumped down and took cover behind the trees on each side of the trail, and there we lay for several minutes, listening to the *brrrrrp-brrrrp* of enemy machine guns and the answering *pop-pop-pop* of E Company's BARs and M1 rifles.

I was once again nearly paralyzed with fear when Rohan ordered those of us armed with M1s and carbines to move out, leaving our gunners and assistant gunners—who carried only pistols—to stay behind with the mortars on the jeeps.

"C'mon, you guys, goddamnit, let's *go!*" Rohan repeated. It was with the greatest reluctance that I forced myself to stand up and tell the equally reluctant Vincent and Packard to follow me with their carbines. Rohan led the three of us past a jeep and an idling Sherman tank toward the sound of the firing. We had gone up only a little way through the trees bordering the trail when the firing abruptly ceased, and we heard several faint German voices shouting, "*Kamerad! Kamerad!*"

A minute or so later we came to a clearing in which a medic knelt by a wounded GI on a stretcher, and down the trail toward us came a group of SS prisoners, hands on heads, accompanied by several E Company riflemen with bayonets affixed to their rifles. These were the first SS troops we had seen, and perhaps it was just my imagination, but they sure did look bigger, tougher, and meaner than any of the German prisoners I had seen to that time. We stepped off the trail to let the stony-faced supermen go past, prodded by the guards. When I saw that several of them had been wounded, I thought, *So much for the rumor that they will fight to the last man or commit suicide rather than surrender. Maybe they're not so tough after all.*

We continued up the trail to another clearing, where we saw our tall, broad-beamed company commander, Captain Neal, talking with Lieutenant Colonel Gettys and a few staff officers. Off to one side, sitting on a stump, sat an arrogant-looking SS officer with one bloody arm nearly shot off, guarded by a rifleman with a bayonet on his rifle. As we filed past, someone behind me said, "Lookit the fancy braid on that sumbitch's shoulder straps! What is he, a general?"

The guard took a drag on his cigarette, threw the butt down, and said disdainfully, "Naw, he's just a major, but he speaks good English. An' if he gives me any more of his crap about callin' a medic to look at his arm, I'm gonna stick him! All our medics is busy lookin' after our own wounded. He kin just sit here an' bleed t' death as far as I'm concerned."

A BADLY WOUNDED SS MAJOR UNDER GUARD

Hearing this, the arrogant major, obviously in great pain, grimaced, looked pleadingly at us, and exclaimed, *"I demand to speak with an officer! It is my right according to the rules!"*

With that, the guard took a threatening step toward him, pointed his bayonet at his belly, and said, "Shut yer goddamn mouth, you!"

Leaving the clearing, we continued on up the narrow trail, in the trace of one of our rifle platoons and our two light-machine-gun squads led by Staff Sergeant Cree. Behind us we could hear the tanks coming. We passed a group of Easy Company riflemen hunkered down behind the trees on either side of the trail.

In an hour or so we came to another large clearing, where the trail intersected a dirt road leading through the forest to the left. Here we stopped for a ten-minute break. While we rested, listening to a smattering of distant small-arms fire to our left rear, a jeep roared up and out stepped Lieutenant Colonel Gettys; Captain Neal; and our company's communications sergeant, whose name was Hanson, carrying his big backpack radio. From where we stood we could hear Gettys talking excitedly into the microphone of Hanson's radio: "Got 'em in the bag, Sid! Fox Company is moving in from the northeast, Howe Company is supporting Easy Company on the west, and I'm taking George Company and the tanks around by road to the southeast to trap 'em."

From his reference to "Sid" we knew that he was talking with our regimental commander, Sidney Wooten.

"Holy shit, didja hear that?" one of the machine gunners ahead of me exclaimed. "Colonel Gettys says we got the bastards in a trap! By God, let's *massacre* the sons a bitches!"

With that, the order came to move out, and a current of excitement passed down the column as we turned left and headed along the dirt road through the trees to the east. Gettys and Neal led the way on foot, setting a fast pace, and the tanks brought up the rear.

· · ·

At about one o'clock that afternoon, the curtain rose on the second act in the drama that was the battle for the Budinger Wald. The dirt road to the east became a sunken lane, with trees and tall bushes growing along the high bank to our left, and more trees and high weeds on the lower bank to our right. Only a little sunlight came through the overhanging tangle of branches and green foliage overhead.

As it turned out, only six members of George Company actually engaged the SS troopers with direct rifle fire that afternoon. The six were Zarimba; his two mortar ammunition bearers; me; and my two ammunition bearers, Vincent and Packard. This little engagement was the first opportunity I had to fire my M1 rifle in anger.

Just before 1:00 P.M. our column had marched along the sunken road to a point at which we could see an open space ahead. Gettys and Neal suddenly signaled a halt. We saw Gettys speak rapidly on the radio again; then we saw the riflemen and the two machine-gun squads led by Cree turn and run back toward where we waited, followed by the two officers and Sergeant Hanson. As Cree ran past, he breathlessly told us that a group of SS troopers were reportedly trying to escape to the south, behind us, and that the rifle platoon and machine-gun squads had been ordered all the way back to where the tanks waited. They were to form a firing line along the top of the high bank, facing north, with the tanks backing them up.

As the red-faced Gettys and the lumbering Neal came puffing up to where we stood, Gettys stopped, gestured wildly at the line of bushes on our left, facing north, and gasped, "Quick, some of you men get up there on that bank and hit the dirt! Form a firing line in those bushes! Keep your eyes on that open field and the hill, and watch the road to the east. Fox Company should be coming over that hill to meet us in half an hour or so. Who's in charge here?"

"Sergeant Rohan is, sir," Neal answered, pointing at Johnny

Rohan. "This is G Company's mortar section. And this other man is Sergeant Bailey. Mortar squad leader."

"Bailey," Gettys nodded. "I remember you. Okay, Rohan, leave five or six of your guys here, get 'em up in those bushes to keep watch. Then you and Bailey and the others follow me and Captain Neal. Get a mortar off the jeep back there and set it up, just in case we need it. Let's go."

Rohan, Bailey, and Bailey's two ammunition bearers followed the two officers back along the sunken road at a trot. Zarimba and I scrambled up the bank, followed by the four ammunition bearers carrying carbines. We moved forward to the edge of the trees and bushes, where we faced a gently sloping hill that rose to a treeless skyline. After the six of us were lying prone, looking out across the field, Zarimba and I used our binoculars to scan the open hillside and the ridge to our north, the distant tree line on our left, and the dirt road to our right.

It was hard for me to use the binoculars with my glasses on. I was sweating, and the lenses fogged up. I cursed silently as I took my glasses off and wiped them with my handkerchief. Then I checked to see that I had a full eight-round clip in my rifle, with one round in the chamber. I brushed some twigs from the damp ground next to my right arm, spread my handkerchief out on the dirt, took two more clips from pouches in my ammunition belt, and lay them on the handkerchief.

Zarimba and his two men were lying prone a few yards to my left, and Vincent and Packard were prone to my right. The surly Packard grumbled when I told him to move right to a better position from which he could keep watch on the road. I could see his lips forming words that I took to be something like, "Piss on you, Joy," and he didn't move. But I nervously snarled at him, saying, "Packard, that's an order! Now move your ass over there where you can see better." He moved.

Just about then, Zarimba whispered hoarsely, "Hey, look there to the left, comin' out of those trees!" I raised up to look where he was pointing, and there at a distance of three or four hundred yards I could just make out a file of men emerging from the woods and heading up the slope in front of us. For the next minute or two the conversation in our little group went something like this:

"Are them guys Krauts or—?"

"Nah, those look like American uniforms to me."

"Maybe that's Fox Company, do ya think?"

"Can't be. Fox is supposed to be coming from over on our right."

I raised my binoculars again to watch the men in the lead come closer as they trudged up the hill, moving across our front from left to right. They began to look more and more like Ger-

WE PREPARE TO OPEN FIRE ON SS TROOPS

mans, from the shape of their helmets. Time stood still. I wished that Rohan was with us to make the decision to open fire. At last, as I focused on the seventh or eighth figure in the column and recognized the unmistakable shape of a German light machine gun on his shoulder, I knew beyond a doubt that they were SS troopers, not Americans.

"They're Krauts—they're Krauts," I croaked at last. "Open fire! Let's hit 'em with everything we got before they spot us and turn that machine gun on us!"

On my right, Vincent's carbine barked first, then I took aim at the figure carrying the machine gun on his shoulder, and squeezed off two quick rounds.

"Shit," Vincent said, "they're way too far away for our carbines!"

I hollered, "You guys with carbines, hold your fire and spot for Zarimba and me. We'll have to hit 'em with our M1s."

I had loaded my two clips so that every other round was a tracer, and I told Vincent, "Watch my tracers; tell me if I'm over or under!"

In the next minute or two, with Vincent spotting where my tracers went, I fired three full eight-round clips at the running, stumbling figures. Zarimba was also firing his M1 as fast as he could.

To my knowledge, the SS troopers never fired a shot at us during that little engagement. In fact, I am sure they never knew from which direction those first shots we fired were coming. We could see the obvious confusion and panic in that line of Germans on the horizon. They were looking this way and that as several of them were hit and fell, including the machine gunner who was my initial target.

I know that at least two of my shots hit the machine gunner, and Vincent told me that I had hit three or four others, who stumbled and dropped to the ground. It was a miracle that just two M1 semiautomatic rifles—Zarimba's and mine—took on what was likely a full platoon of SS troops, probably killing or wounding at least a dozen. The battle was not quite over, however, when Zarimba and I ceased firing.

Just as I was about to suggest that we had better get the hell back down the bank and out of sight before some of the now-prone SS troops opened fire on our position, we heard the *pop-pop-pop, pop-pop-pop* of BAR fire coming from our right. Seconds later we saw several SS troopers stand up and raise their hands over their heads as they turned to face a skirmish line of Fox Company troops coming over the top of a slight rise on our right. We watched the skirmishers advance down the slope to where the surviving SS were surrendering.

Then we heard one of our tanks noisily coming down the sunken road behind us, and Johnny Rohan scrambled up over the bank and said, "Cease fire—they're surrendering."

My guess is that this action had lasted less than half an hour. If so, it would have been about 1:30 P.M. on that warm afternoon of Tuesday, April 3, 1945, when what turned out to be the massacre of a full company of SS troops ended.

The intrepid Johnny Rohan crouched down beside me where I lay, and when the tank came growling up the bank over on our right he said, "C'mon, Joy, let's go over there with the tank and help F Company make sure all those Krauts are disarmed. Zarimba, you and the rest of you guys stay here and keep us covered."

At first I wanted to decline Rohan's invitation to go out into that killing field to see what we had done. But I knew that he was determined to go by himself, if necessary, so I reluctantly stood up, put a fresh clip in my rifle, slung my binoculars around my neck, and nodded that I was ready. Rohan waved a "Come on, follow us" gesture to the tank commander, who had his head out of the turret hatch, and he waved back, signaling that he would follow.

I felt numb and sick to my stomach as I followed Rohan out into that open field. I held my rifle at the ready with its safety off, and I tried not to look too closely at the inert bodies of several SS troopers; I kept my eyes mainly on the long line of other Germans farther up the slope, standing with their hands up, as the F Company skirmishers frisked them.

CHECKING WOUNDED AS SS TROOPS SURRENDER

Rohan was several yards ahead, off to my right, and I turned to make sure the tank was following us. Just as I turned forward again, out of the corner of my eye I saw a big SS trooper, who lay on his back with helmet off and left arm outstretched, move his other arm up to his face, holding something in his hand. I froze, raised my rifle, and thought, *The bastard has a hand grenade!*

Before I could squat down and take aim, I heard the tank

stop just behind me, and I turned to see a short black guy wearing a tanker's helmet and sergeant's stripes drop down from the turret and come running up behind me. He was carrying a tommy gun, and fired a short three-round burst past me into the side of the German. The big SS trooper jerked, flopped over, and dropped whatever was in his hand.

The sergeant and I walked up cautiously, and I saw what looked like a very dull mess kit knife near the SS trooper's hand. Then I noticed a bloodless deep cut across his white throat, and knew he had been trying to slit his throat with the knife. Dumbfounded, shaking my head, I turned away and headed to where Rohan stood talking with one of the F Company sergeants. Before I had gone ten paces I heard the tank sergeant behind me snarl, "Still breathin', ya bastard? Okay, now die!"

And as I watched, unable to say anything, the angry little sergeant leaned over the SS trooper's body and shot him again with another short burst from his tommy gun. Of all the sights I saw during my days in combat, that was one of the worst. It was an atrocity, pure and simple, and had an officer seen it happen, God knows what might have been done to that sergeant. I dared say nothing to his scowling face as he glared at me as if to say, *Ya wanna make somethin' of it?*

I was so sickened and ashamed that my memory of what happened during the remainder of that day, before the sun went down, is a blank. But I do remember sitting on guard in a foxhole for several hours that cold night, acting as an assistant machine gunner in one of our company outposts, while a rifle squad moved out on night patrol.

During those dark hours guarding our perimeter, my companion in the two-man foxhole—one of our machine gunners—listened as I told him about the tank sergeant who had twice shot the dying SS trooper. Then I mentioned the badly wounded SS major who earlier that morning had been so arrogantly demanding to speak with an officer.

"Yeah, ya know what happened to him, doncha?" my companion whispered.

"No, what?" I replied. "He bled to death?"

"Hell, no. After all them guys surrendered, one of our medics came out there to take a look. He told me that when he finally got around to give that major a shot of morphine, the bastard was so snotty he gave him an extra needle. Killed him in a minute."

How many more such atrocities may have been committed by American GIs that day on the battlefield of the Budinger Wald is anybody's guess. Those are the two cases I know about firsthand.

Here is what *The History of the U.S. Army 71st Infantry Division* has to say about the battle for Budinger Wald:

> Early on April 1 information was received that approximately 700 enemy troops were entering the Division's zone. Contact was made with the enemy on that date by the 71st Reconnaissance Troop. A battalion of the 14th Combat Team then moved to the vicinity of Altenstadt, split the enemy forces and caused them to disperse into a heavily wooded area. PWs taken were identified as members of the 6th SS Mountain Division Nord.
>
> The next day, April 2, the Second and Third Battalions of the 14th Infantry launched a coordinated attack supported by artillery, tanks, and tank destroyers. The Second Battalion of the 66th Infantry, reinforced with tanks, and infantry cannon, established a block to the south and east to catch SSers attempting to escape in that direction.
>
> In the meantime, because the Division had the multiple mission of protecting the Corps' right flank, its rear and vul-

nerable left flank, the 5th Infantry, reinforced, was committed in order to clear the main route as quickly as possible.

Early on April 2, the 5th seized Buches and Budingen, and coordinated its attack with the 14th Infantry. Pressure continued on April 3 driving the 6th SS Division into Budinger Wald to the east. Roadblocks, established to the north and northeast, completed the encirclement. Combined action by all the units concerned, Infantry, Artillery, Tanks, Tank Destroyers, and Cavalry, brought about complete destruction and capture of the 6th SS Division. 2,700 SSers were taken prisoner by the 71st in this action.

On Wednesday, April 4, we climbed out of our foxholes and headed northeast through several more small patches of woods. On this date my squad of five men was converted to what Captain Neal called an assault squad. The highlights of what happened that day are summarized in my little notebook: "We reorganize, my squad becomes an assault squad. We leave Mortars on Jeep, Carry 1 Bazooka and 1 AR. Sweep woods, 2 ridges. Rohan makes Jerry prisoners (young boys) goosestep and Drill. That afternoon a BAR man of rifle platoon kills and wounds 2 Germans. Heinies were asleep. Hike on. Billet in house with Arm'd Cavalry."

From April 4 until the war in Europe ended thirty-four days later, we moved fast with Patton's Third Army through the heart of Germany and on to the southeast into Bavaria, then into Austria. We marched mostly on foot, but sometimes rode on half-tracks, or on the top of tanks, or in six-by-six trucks.

April 4 was our twenty-sixth day in combat, and every day we came under fire, usually from snipers in the woods, sometimes from mortars or artillery, and a few times from strafing fighter planes of the Luftwaffe. Every day we captured prisoners—sometimes only a handful, at other times hundreds.

CHAPTER 18

A LETTER HOME, THE WAREHOUSE AT FULDA, AND ON TO COBURG

Thursday, April 5, through Wednesday, April 11, 1945

On April 5 we rode on half-tracks belonging to the 14th Armored Cavalry Squadron, and sometime before 5:00 P.M. we reached the outskirts of Fulda, where we spent the night in a large house. There I found time to write a long letter home. It was the first of my letters in which I was, apparently, in a philosophical mood:

Dear folks,

Just arrived at another town (have been located at 5 or 6 different stops—towns and woods since I last wrote). About an hour ago, got my insides well-heated with a big double dose of C ration coffee after a long & rough & cold ride atop a halftrack, and now I'm well situated in a warm room all ready to write a good letter to you.

Guess it must be 3 or 4 days since I last wrote, so must bring you up to date. We are now in the 3rd Army. I may've told you that already—I can't remember for sure. We haven't run into much heavy resistance ourselves, as old "Blood & Guts" [Patton] always seems to be way out ahead 2 or 3 days, with his Tankers, but we have been seeing a scrap daily for the last few days, and I guarantee you I've been walking my poor old legs off.

I imagine you folks at home have been pretty happy with the news of the several breakthroughs over here, & perhaps you expect it to end shortly—in fact, we read in the S. & S. [Stars & Stripes] recently that the U.S. celebrated a false-reported surrender for 20 minutes, a few days ago. Well, I would not be at all shocked if most resistance had ceased before this ever reaches you—but I know from recent first hand experiences that these SS troopers are "problem boys"—lots of them don't believe in surrendering as you've probably heard. And we may still be mopping them up for a long long while. I hope not. I don't want to be pessimistic, but don't expect everything to be peaceful over here after it's over.

It's really no fun even just being over here, in this messed up land of Germany, notwithstanding [I surely meant "not to mention"] having to help kill & capture. The whole darn country & people & circumstances we are in don't help in forming healthy states of mind in ourselves, but we are doing our best to stay happy & content. The Germans don't like us one bit—many of them hate us very much. You've heard about the Army's non-fraternization policy & the heavy penalties for violation, have you not? It is very necessary, for the success of our mission—which is to remold the minds of these unfortunate people. Success of this plan is also very dependent on our not feeling sorry for any of them, or showing sympathy toward any of them—all a part of non-fraternization—(I hear the "Beer Barrel Polka" playing on a record machine in one of the other squad's rooms).

You may be thinking it is hard for me to be like that—a guy who never smiles at a German, who treats them courteous but firm—and who truly, deep down inside, feels sorry for none ex-

cepting those who can't be blamed. (Have to change to German red ink now—am out of blue & can't find any around).

And those who I feel can't be blamed for anything are the young children, and the very old people. I never thought I'd get to the point where a woman in tears wouldn't even phase me, but that doesn't bother any of us over here.

Now, I realize, from reading your recent letters Kathie [I called my sister Kathleen *Kathie* back then] *that you and I will not agree on some of these things, but as I see it that is no fault of either of us—it is the result of each of us having our own opinions & beliefs formed, & the fact that at present we are living in 2 "worlds" so vastly different that neither can really truly understand the other's side of it. Until we can discuss it with actual words instead of bridging the distance between our 2 worlds with letters, I doubt if you'll see my side of it, or I'll see yours.*

Let me say here that, although what I said about conscientious objectors was my true feeling, this war will never make one out of me. Certainly war is not right. But it's the only way for us at present, for you see, these German people do not think, talk, or understand the language of equality, kindness, generousity, compassion. All they understand is the language of cruel force. That's the language we must talk.

And what must God think about it? Well, who started this war? Certainly not Him. We human beings did—yes, I feel we Americans are to blame as much as anyone. For we've had the God-given opportunities to put across to the less fortunate people on this earth the fundamentals of living peacefully, and I guess we failed. Therefore we were forced to fight. We're fighting for another chance to show them the light. I admit that what "light" we Americans have had and will have to show has been feeble, but it's still probably the brightest of all, as it is newer. As I see it, War itself is not so much a sin in itself, as it is a part of a big sin (or maybe the result or punishment for a sin)—that big sin being our failure mentioned above.

*One thing I've always wondered about and will always won-
der about until I get an answer that satisfies me completely, is:
why were we the lucky ones to be born Americans—to receive,
without even working for it, the benefit of such a land of
plenty—to be born right into a high standard of living such as is
ours? Did you ever really wonder about that? Did you ever wonder why you weren't born a German, or a Jap, to grow up with
the ideals they have? Or born a pygmie (correct spelling?) in
Africa, living a primitive life? The only answer I've yet formed in
my mind to those questions (and I'm still not sure it's the right
one or the complete one) is that I must be part of God's plan—
the "God's plan" that you spoke about in your letter, Mother.*

*Well, I've used up quite a lot of ink, paper, & energy, & time
on the subject so will drop it for now. I'm fine.*

> *Love,*
> *Dean*

That night my squad and I were called out to guard a nearby
hospital full of Germans. On the next day, Friday, April 6, I
began to record the passwords in my little notebook. These were
changed every morning. Whether the passwords were common
throughout all of the U.S. armies in Europe, or whether each division had its own, I am not sure, but I expect it was the former.
There were always two passwords. When any of us was challenged by a sentry, especially at night, we whispered the first
word, and the sentry then established that he was friendly by answering with the second word.

My notebook entry for April 6 was brief: "Password
{Dagwood-Bumper}. Guard warehouse full of food for the Wer-
macht. Boy, do we eat!"

For some reason this entry neglected to even hint at the scary
and unusual night three of us spent guarding a dark and lonely
warehouse on the western outskirts of Fulda. Captain Neal gave
the order to either Rohan or Cree to send three men back to the

warehouse in a jeep. Rohan told me to choose two others from my newly formed assault squad and go. I chose Hatley and Vincent, now armed with M1 rifles, and left Decker and Packard behind with our bazooka and BAR. It is a mystery to me why I didn't bring the BAR.

It must have been an hour or so before nightfall when one of G Company's two jeeps picked us up in front of our house. The warehouse was a long, rectangular, windowless metal structure on a rural road in a large, open field, with no farmhouses or trees nearby. It had a loading dock and large sliding doors facing the road. The nearest houses were at least half a mile to the east, on the road leading back to Fulda. I am amazed that we had no radio to call for help in case of an attack.

We were told only that the warehouse was full of rations for the Wehrmacht and that we were to guard it until dawn, as there might be a few hungry civilians or straggling soldiers in the woods to the north who might try to break in during the night. A unit from our regimental service company would come out after daybreak to take over, and the company jeep would pick us up and bring us back to Fulda. We were also told that a squad of our division engineers had checked the place for mines and booby traps and had found none. After the jeep dropped us off and headed back to Fulda, we took a quick walk around the outside and found that the only other entrance was a small, heavily padlocked and barred door in back. It didn't take me long to decide that it made no sense for three GIs armed with M1s and hand grenades to try to guard that warehouse from the outside. That would have taken at least a full squad, if not a platoon. What would Johnny Rohan do if he were with us?

We opened one of the two front sliding doors just far enough for one man at a time to enter. Using our flashlights, we discovered that the dark cavern was filled almost to the ceiling girders with stacks of wooden boxes of different sizes—each box stenciled with German words indicating either canned goods, butter, or marmalade. Just inside the doors was an empty rectangular space on the cement floor, measuring perhaps thirty feet wide by twenty feet deep. There were boxes stacked to the left and right of this space, and a single aisle about seven or eight feet wide led all the way back to the rear door, between other high stacks.

We cautiously walked down that aisle, looking for trip wires or any sign that there might be booby traps, even though our engineers had supposedly checked for these already. We found nothing that looked suspicious to our untrained eyes, so we returned to the open rectangular area in the front and I made a decision. I said: "Okay, guys, we'll all spend the night right here. We're not gonna split up. Let's pile some more boxes up in front of that aisle and make ourselves a little fort, just in case. Two of us can sleep while one is on watch."

The boxes were heavy. We pulled the lids off of several. One box contained cans of sardines. Another had some kind of crackers in cans. Another contained butter—it may have been margarine—in smaller wooden boxes. And a fourth box had marmalade, also in smaller wooden boxes.

It was still light outside when we finished building our little fortress of boxes, then sat down to sample the sardines, crackers, butter, and marmalade, courtesy of the Wehrmacht. I guess that meal is why I made the last entry in my diary for that day, "Boy, do we eat!" Then, as it began to get dark and cold, Vincent had what I thought was a brilliant idea: He suggested that to keep warm, we should build a small fire in our little enclosure, using the thin strips of wood that had been the box covers, and some of the splintered smaller boxes that had contained butter and marmalade. That is exactly what we did. We figured that the high ceiling would allow the smoke to disperse, and if the fire was kept small enough, there was no danger of the stacks of boxes catching fire. I also figured that if we heard anyone trying to break in the barred door at the far end of the dark aisle, we could douse the fire quickly.

SCARY NIGHT GUARDING A GERMAN WAREHOUSE

After the fire was started, I took Vincent outside with me, told Hatley to close the sliding door leading out to the loading dock, and the two of us checked to make sure none of the firelight could be seen from the front of the warehouse. Satisfied, we rejoined Hatley inside, and unrolled our three sleeping bags close together on the concrete floor, with our little bonfire and a small stack of splintered wood just within reach in front of us. Hatley lay on my left and Vincent on my right, with our rifles resting on boxes in front of us. We heated instant C ration coffee in our canteen cups, and talked in whispers for a while.

"If anyone tries to get in that rear door," I said, "let's all of us open up with our M1s, rapid fire. We'll each fire two full clips.

Aim up at the ceiling and down that aisle to the back. That'll make 'em think we're a full battalion and scare 'em off."

At about 9:00 P.M. I set the guard duty schedule. Each of us in turn was to stay awake for an hour, then sleep for two hours. I took the first watch, from nine to ten, followed by Hatley for an hour, then Vincent, who would wake me for the fourth watch, at midnight. Except for the crackling of our little fire and maybe a few snores from the two sleepers, the hours passed in silence. It was hard to keep my eyes open, but I managed with the help of a second cup of coffee. I slept from ten to midnight, was awake from midnight until 1:00 A.M., then was relieved again by Hatley.

Some time between 2:00 and 3:00 A.M., as I was sleeping soundly, Vincent shook me awake and whispered, "Listen! I hear something! Douse the fire!"

I listened, and from down the aisle I could hear a *rattle-rattle*-pause-*rattle-rattle-rattle*. I woke Hatley with my elbow, and the three of us frantically put out the fire with water from our canteens, clicked the safeties off of our M1s, and waited. Again there came a persistent *rattle-rattle-rattle*. I whispered, "Okay, guys, open fire. Everyone fire two clips."

Talk about an ear-splitting noise! Those forty-eight rounds we fired in the next half minute were very much amplified by the enclosed warehouse, and when we ceased fire my ears were ringing. I wished that I had worn cotton in my ears, as we had usually done back on the Fort Benning firing ranges. We each reloaded a fresh clip in our rifles and waited—and waited—and grinned at each other sheepishly for what we had done. And for the rest of that night we all stayed awake. But there were no more noises.

Just after dawn the next morning, Saturday, April 7, we cautiously slid the door behind us open, and shortly thereafter we saw a jeep coming down the road from Fulda, followed by two five-ton trucks. I decided it wouldn't be smart to divulge the full story of how we had built a fire and opened up with our rifles when we heard the noises, so I told Hatley and Vincent to scatter the ashes and pick up our empty cartridge cases. Then we quickly stuffed a few cans of sardines and crackers and some marmalade boxes into our packs, rolled up our sleeping bags, strapped them onto our packs, and waited.

When the jeep pulled up, we recognized Captain Neal's driver behind the wheel, and next to him sat a young officer from our regimental service company. After he got out and motioned for the two trucks to back up to the dock, he asked me how our night had gone. I told him only that we had been cold as hell, that we had heard a few noises at the rear door, but the noises had lasted only a minute or two. Then I suggested we walk around back to investigate. And sure enough, there in the soft turf around the padlocked rear door, and along a path leading north to the distant line of trees, we saw several muddy footprints—some coming and some going—made by hobnailed boots. That fusillade of rifle shots we had fired had not been such a dumb idea after all.

Safely back in our house at Fulda, we ate a breakfast of C rations, German sardines, and marmalade spread on crackers. Then we slept. That afternoon, Rohan woke me up and whispered, "The Grimy One is in the front room to see you."

"Top? Sergeant Anderson?" I asked, thinking, *Oh-oh, trouble about last night.* I wondered why else our First Sergeant would want to see me. But old Top was all smiles as he said, "Congratulations, Sergeant Joy, Captain Neal's givin' ya three stripes."

Everyone shook my hand, and Rohan gave me two or three sets of buck sergeant stripes to sew on my shirt and field jacket—he now wore the three stripes and rocker of a staff sergeant. From what I wrote in my little notebook that afternoon or the next morning, I guess it must have been payday, and we all probably went to the company CP to line up while one of the officers doled out our pay, in German script. My brief entry reads as follows: "7 April Made Sgt. Payday. Guard Warehouse again."

It was a different, multistory warehouse right in Fulda that we guarded that night.

Sunday, April 8, was not a day of rest; we moved east from Fulda, partly on foot and partly riding on trucks. The next two days, April 9 and 10, nothing much happened. Wednesday, April 11, was our thirty-third day in combat. We rode trucks to the outskirts of Coburg, and that night was one of the most frightening of all the nights spent in foxholes during my time as a combat infantryman.

CHAPTER 19

COBURG, BAYREUTH, PEGNITZ, AND A ROADBLOCK IN THE FOREST

Thursday, April 12, through Friday, April 20, 1945

There was a large, open field on the northwestern outskirts of Coburg, bounded on the south by a forest that rose to a long ridge running east and west. This forested ridge was about fifteen miles long. The field was bounded on the southwest by the forest and a dirt road from a village called Rodach, some nine miles west of Coburg, and on the east by a paved highway coming south from another village, called Rottenbach.

On the night of April 11–12, the entire 5th-Infantry Regiment of some three thousand men, and probably two hundred to three hundred vehicles—jeeps, trucks, and tanks—were jam-packed into this open field, with the regiment's three rifle battalions in foxholes around the southeastern perimeter. The plan was that our regiment would attack Coburg on the morning of April 12, supported by a full battalion of tanks and no less than *nine* battalions of field artillery—more than a hundred 105mm and 155mm howitzers and 8-inchers. The word was passed that old Blood and Guts Patton himself had ordered this massive concentration of artillery.

On the division and regimental maps, I imagine that this bivouac and the positions of the nine supporting artillery battalions must have formed a large kidney-shaped area around the north, northwest, and west of the city of Coburg. My squad's foxholes were in the southern part of that bivouac, but just before dark, Johnny Rohan came over to where I was cleaning my rifle and gave me some unwelcome news. We would *not* spend the night in the foxholes we had just dug.

"Why not, John?" I asked.

"Because you and your squad got the job to set up a listening post tonight," he explained. "There may be some Kraut patrols coming down the hill through that forest to probe our positions after dark. This afternoon two jeeps from H Company got ambushed in a small village not far up the road to the west where it disappears into those woods."

My five-man squad included Decker, Hatley, Vincent, Packard, and myself, but the entry in my little notebook says that six of us were sent out to that listening post in the edge of the woods. I am not sure who the sixth man was—I think he may have been someone from our company communications section with a reel of wire and a sound-power telephone, as that was standard practice for listening posts. If it was, it is certain that the phone connection back to the company perimeter didn't work.

We left our foxholes just after dark. I checked in with a squad of riflemen whose foxholes were within the company perimeter closest to the line of trees we had been told to go to. I wanted to make sure they knew we were out there in case we had to run back through their position, and that they knew that the passwords for that night were "Sara-Lou."

Our newly formed *assault* squad was armed with three M1 rifles, a BAR, and a bazooka. We probably had two or three antitank bazooka rockets with us. We wore only light combat packs, and each of us had either a folding shovel or a pick. It was just light enough to see when we crossed the dirt road and climbed up a low embankment along the edge of the trees. The sky was clear, no rain was expected, and it promised to be a fairly warm spring night, so we had not brought raincoats—just our field jackets.

We moved cautiously and quietly a few yards up the slope and through the trees above the road, and came across several logs lying in what looked like might once have been a logging trail. I decided this was a good place to hunker down and set up our position, and everyone agreed. The narrow little trail was slightly sunken, not as deep as a foxhole or a slit trench, but the logs gave us some protection all around, and the last thing any of us wanted to do was to make noise digging foxholes, which would give away our position.

I placed Hatley, who carried the BAR, facing uphill to the south behind one of the logs. Decker with his M1 was on Hatley's left, with extra magazines for the BAR. And just in case a German tank or armored car came along the road from the west, I placed Vincent and our bazooka behind a log facing that direction, with Packard and his M1 next to him. I covered the eastern approach with my M1, lying behind a log and looking down along the little logging trail in the direction of Coburg. To my left, looking north down toward the open field, was the sixth man, whoever he was. Three of us stayed awake at all times while the other three tried to sleep.

Sleep came hard for me. I kept hearing mysterious noises from the woods above us, and every now and then one of the men would whisper something like, "*Hey, Sarge, didja hear that noise?*"

Perhaps a slight breeze was blowing from the north, because sounds from the company perimeter, at least a hundred yards north of us, reached our ears. Now and then we heard a truck tailgate slam, or an engine start up as some vehicle moved its po-

OUR LISTENING POST OVERLOOKING COBURG BIVOUAC

sition, and I remember the constant *chug-chug-chug* of what was probably a small diesel generator. There may have been some moonlight, because I could just make out the dark outline of some of the larger trucks. To the east we could see one or two spires of the churches in Coburg.

It must have been about two o'clock in the morning when those of us who were awake heard a sudden high voice from the perimeter shout, *"Halt!"* A few seconds later came a louder, more insistent *"HALT!"* And then all hell seemed to break loose out in that field where the 5th Infantry Regiment was dug in. First a tommy gun opened up with its distinctive short bursts, then two or three BARs and one of our machine guns. There were all kinds of colored tracers flying every which way. A few of the tracers came in our direction, and I whispered something like, "Watch it, guys! If that's a Kraut patrol they may be bugging out this way."

And then we saw a small flame and heard a *pop*, and in a few seconds we could see that one of the big trucks just to the left of George Company's position had started to burn. We all figured that a tracer from one of the trigger-happy American sentries had hit the truck's gas tank, and now we could see a large part of the field lit up by the growing conflagration. Someone close to the burning truck hollered, "Everyone in their holes! Everyone in their holes!"

It seemed like maybe a dozen or more voices out in that field picked up the cry "*Everyone in their holes!*" and in another few seconds we understood why. There was a bright flash and a loud explosion, followed immediately by several more, and in the light I could make out several short-barreled 105mm howitzers parked near the truck, and knew that the truck must be loaded with shells for the regimental cannon company.

That truck burned for what must have been half an hour, and there came repeated loud blasts of more shells going off. Once or twice bits and pieces of that truck and a few splinters of shrapnel flew overhead, as far as our position. Of course we kept our heads down behind the logs, but soon we began to worry more about how the light from those flames would silhouette us for any Germans who might be close by in the woods above our position.

After the flames died down and there were no more explosions, someone—it might have been Packard—suggested that it might be a good idea to run back to the safety of George Company's perimeter. But I turned that idea down, much as I, too, wanted to get out of our exposed position.

Our little adventure ended just after dawn, when Rohan led Bailey's and Zarimbas's squads out to where we lay, and told us to get some coffee and have breakfast. Then we were to come back out and join Bailey and Zarimba for a reconnaissance patrol up the hill into the woods. As far as I know, there were only a few minor casualties when Cannon Company's ammo truck was hit and blew up during the night.

Sometime after noon we returned from that morning patrol, which involved a tense sweep of the woods. We learned that the mayor of Coburg and a few of his officials had been escorted, under a white flag, to the field where the regiment was deployed, and had been shown the nine battalions of field artillery that were ready to plaster the city. They had then been sent back with an ultimatum for the commander of the SS troops said to be holding out in the center of town. The ultimatum said, in effect: "Tell the commander he has one hour to surrender, or at least to evacuate all his troops from the city, or we will level the place with artillery!"

We were told that George Patton himself had set this new policy for using artillery on any town or city that refused to surrender, or from which snipers fired on American troops when they entered, especially after seeing white flags flying from windows and steeples. This, it was said, had been happening all too frequently.

In that regard, we also learned that another patrol had been sent into the little town up in the woods to the west, where our H Company jeeps had been ambushed the previous afternoon. It was said that this patrol had captured or killed several of the snipers.

Just after our cold lunch, we learned that Coburg had indeed surrendered and the SS troops had departed under the dire threat of a massive artillery attack. We were ordered to pack up and load on trucks for the ride into the city.

Sometime that evening we learned what had really happened with the other patrol that had gone up into the little village to the west that morning. The story came from one of our rifle platoons, which had been led back to the village by the H Company lieutenant whose men had been ambushed and killed by the snipers.

It seems the patrol had crawled into that town through a deep drainage ditch, had surrounded the building or buildings from which the snipers had fired, and had shortly captured several of these Germans. The lieutenant, with tears streaming down his face, told his interpreter to order the prisoners to line up, turn their backs, and drop their pants, upon which he had personally shot them all down with his tommy gun. Several of us knew that H Company lieutenant by sight and name, but inasmuch as we had not been witnesses to the crime, there was nothing we could do. The story seems to have been true, because Captain Neal later read us a message from our division commander, addressed to all troops, warning that crimes such as this were punishable by death.

Friday was April 13, and although I have always been superstitious about that combination, I didn't catch the fact when I wrote my next notebook entry. But that *was* the day we learned of President Roosevelt's unexpected death.

A few desultory sniper shots were fired at us from long range that afternoon, when we arrived at a little farm village southeast of Coburg. The civilians in that village complained when we kicked them out of their houses and told them to spend the night in a large barn. And to make that unlucky Friday complete, that night we were all infested with lice from the farmer's straw ticks on which we unthinkingly slept. The next morning, Saturday, we were in misery, but thanks to one of our medics, we powdered ourselves and our clothes liberally with DDT. My notebook entry for that day reads: "14 April Password {Class-School} Rode Tanks, wild ride, to another town—Merriott cooks a big meal for us. Found 120 Dozen eggs!! Two lost GIs from 14th Arm'd Div join us."

I well remember that wild ride atop the tank. We went from village to village, now and then hearing distant rifle shots and poised to jump off if the tank drew fire. Luckily, it didn't.

Once we stopped near a farmhouse where the tank commander had spotted several chickens in the backyard. In a jiffy the tank commander and his gunner were out of that tank and up in the yard. They captured three or four hens and wrung their necks, as the German farm woman tore her hair and shrieked what were probably vile curses.

En route to the next little village, where we finally were let off, we heard goings-on inside the tank turret. At the next stop we were amazed to find out that the tankers had been boiling water in a large kettle as we moved. When the tank stopped and all five crewmen dismounted, they plucked those chickens clean, dumped two of them in the big kettle set over their little gasoline stove, and wonder of wonders, they gave *us* the third chicken! Nice guys, those tankers! We gave them some of the eggs we had been able to carry with us.

That night, in another old farmhouse where we slept, Decker, Hatley, Vincent, Packard, and I feasted on boiled chicken and hard-boiled eggs. And we had more eggs again for breakfast the next morning, Sunday, April 15.

After our experience with lice the previous night, we did *not* sleep in any of the beds in that farmhouse on the night of April 14–15, nor use any of the heavy quilted comforters we found there. My notebook entry for Sunday reads: "15 April, Password {Griddle-Pan}. Sweep woods all day & round up civilians in 3 or 4 towns, a few prisoners. Billet good—my squad has house all our own."

Although the note does not mention it, I am certain that we slept in the town of Kulmbach that night. The next morning our 2d Battalion went into reserve for two days, and was sent back to guard XII Corps headquarters in the city of Kronach. Because of this assignment we were lucky to miss the battle for the famous

German city of Bayreuth. Another battalion of our regiment was attached to the 14th Armored Division and suffered several casualties in that attack. There was a sneak night air raid by the Luftwaffe, during which our sister battalion was bombed and strafed. George Company also was strafed by a lone German fighter plane, probably part of the same group that attacked Bayreuth.

My notebook entry for Tuesday reads: "17 April Password {Arrow-Head}. 1000 Bombers go over. Move is snafued, we change billet to a barn, see picture 'Here Come The Waves.' "

AWESOME 1,000-PLANE RAID FLIES OVER KRONACH

Those thousand B-17s of the Eighth Air Force were an awesome sight as they thundered east over our heads, probably at about twenty thousand feet. I wanted to mention them in a letter I wrote that afternoon, but Rohan cautioned me that it would be censored, so I left it out. One paragraph from that letter mentions something that I treasure more than any other medal: "I forgot to tell you I've been authorized to wear the Combat Infantryman's Badge. You've no doubt seen it worn. It's silver on blue background. Means nothing much more than that I've seen combat."

On Wednesday, April 18—our fortieth day in combat—we rode trucks from Kronach for more than twenty-five miles to the city of Bayreuth, parts of which were still burning as a result of artillery fire. I remember little of the sights as we passed through that fabled Wagnerian city. Around noon we arrived at an open field surrounded by thick woods. We bitched a bit when we were told that the woods had to be swept that afternoon. There were a few desultory shots fired at us, but we captured no prisoners.

The next day, Thursday, we once again rode in a convoy of trucks another ten miles or so to Pegnitz, a picturesque valley town on a small river. When a few shots were fired at us as we drove into the town center, the trucks immediately stopped to let us off. Several squads, including my own, were ordered to head up the winding side streets, and near the end of the street we searched we came upon a schoolhouse in which we found not snipers, but refugee kids unattended by teachers.

Proceeding on to where the paved road ended, we saw two suspicious-looking farmhouses, one on the left and one on the right. I told Decker, Hatley, and Packard to check out the farmhouse on the left while Vincent and I headed up to the gate of the one on the right. Suddenly a huge German shepherd dog rushed at us, barking angrily.

Vincent and I were carrying our rifles slung on our shoulders, but each of us also had a holstered .45-caliber automatic pistol. As the dog lunged for Vincent, he pulled his automatic, chambered a round with his left hand by pulling back the slide, and fired a shot into the dirt in front of the brute. The dog ran off, unhurt but yelping, and then I heard Vincent swear. "God-damn Sarge, I shot myself!" he exclaimed.

Sure enough, the fleshy part of his left hand, between thumb and forefinger, was bleeding from a deep gash with powder burns on it. As he had released the slide, his left hand moved just forward of the muzzle, and he squeezed the trigger too soon, so that the slug went through the flesh before it hit the dirt. I bandaged his hand with his first-aid kit and sent him back to see our medics. The rest of us made a quick search of both farmhouses, then decided to head back ourselves.

By our forty-second day in combat, which was Friday, April 20, I had begun to believe that I would survive this awful war in which so many of my friends and acquaintances had been killed or badly wounded. One of the ways I kept my spirits up and my mind off of my possible death was to carry on imagined conversations with my father as we marched along the roads between towns. Perhaps because I was now a sergeant leading a squad of men, two of whom were older than I, I had begun to feel a need to show someone my knowledge of tactics and strategy. Or maybe I was remembering the times my dad had taken me out on the eastern Colorado prairie to hunt jackrabbits and cottontails, and had taught me how to carry the little .22 Winchester rifle he had given me, and warned me to keep the safety on. Or maybe I was just thinking of what I would write in my next letter home.

As we marched, I would imagine that my father was beside me, and I would tell him what we were doing, what we were about to do, and explain how we would do it.

See, Dad? I would say silently. *See how well we combat infantrymen have all learned to march, in two columns, one on either side of the road, to let vehicles pass? At this rate we are making more than three miles per hour, and every hour we usually have a ten-minute break. Some days like this we have marched for ten or twelve hours, and covered twenty-five to thirty miles.*

*See how we keep five-yard intervals just in case some ar-
tillery should come in on us, or a German plane should suddenly
make a strafing run? And see those woods up ahead? That's
where the diehard Kraut snipers or machine gunners may be
lying in wait for us. When we get there we will deploy off this
road into a skirmish line. And Dad, notice that even when
marching, I always keep a round in the chamber of my M1 rifle.
But don't worry, I am always careful to keep the safety on.*

During our long march that Friday, one such reverie was suddenly broken by a shot. Not just any old shot, but one that I
thought had hit the stock of my rifle, which I carried slung over
my shoulder. My ears rang, and it was only a second or so before
I realized that it was *my own rifle* that had gone off! What happened was that the protruding "tee" on my bayonet, which hung
from my belt, had somehow caught in my rifle's trigger guard,
clicked off the safety ahead of the trigger, and then as I took another step, it had pulled the trigger.

Everyone in the marching column jumped at the sound and
hit the dirt in the ditches alongside the road—all except me, that
is. I knew what had happened. Our platoon leader, Lieutenant
Joseph Tyler, got up out of the ditch, looked back, and asked,
"Who fired that shot?"

"Me, sir," I said, and explained what had happened.

"Well, Joy, be careful, goddamn it, and don't let that happen
again."

"Yes, sir; I mean, no, sir."

I felt sheepish as the four members of my squad razzed me,
and Tyler went up the line to report to the captain.

At about noon on April 20 we came to a farmhouse in which
we again found a box filled with dozens upon dozens of eggs.
They were floating in a viscous, transparent fluid someone said
was called water glass. My dictionary calls it sodium silicate and
says that this syrupy liquid is often used to preserve eggs.

Although the entire G Company mortar section—now reorganized into three assault squads—was crowded into that little farmhouse, I somehow got the job of supervising the boiling of a big bucket of hot water and hard-boiling several dozen eggs before we had to leave. Just after noon the job was almost finished, and I began passing out the hot eggs from two bowls. Somebody's walkie-talkie radio came to life with Captain Neal's voice saying, "Fourth Platoon, load up, get your asses on the road! We got a bunch of Krauts in the woods down here at a roadblock!"

Everyone in the room rushed to grab as many eggs as they could and stuff them into their field jacket pockets, and before I bolted out the door I, too, grabbed four or five from one of the bowls. I stuffed them in my upper left field jacket pocket, grabbed my rifle, and followed the rest of my squad out the door. Down the road a bit my squad was ordered to take the point and head down a narrow trail leading into the woods to our left. Cree and Rohan led Bailey's and Zarimba's squads and our two machine-gun squads across the road. Just behind them was Captain Neal, his radioman, and a rifle squad.

The firefight at the log roadblock began with a sudden burst from a burp gun. We could see Cree run up to a tree, crouch down, aim, and fire. A German behind another tree, not ten yards to his front, yelped as he was hit. The German's helmet flew off and he toppled out from behind his tree.

As I hit the dirt, I felt the eggs in my left breast pocket break. I had mistakenly grabbed several raw eggs, and now I felt the sticky mess oozing out all over my field jacket. God, did I swear. And it was not until after the war had ended, some eighteen days later, that I finally got my gunky field jacket washed.

After a few minutes I told my squad, "Let's go," and we got up to advance along the trail through the trees. Almost immediately another machine gun opened fire, and we hit the dirt again. Someone fired back, and we saw a helmeted Kraut roll away from his machine gun, whose barrel protruded from some bushes behind a small log. We advanced cautiously, and the five of us knelt down by the wounded German. Packard pulled the biggest revolver I have ever seen from his belt, put the muzzle against the German's temple, and asked, "Kin ah shoot this sumbitch, Joy?"

"Christ, no, you dumb bastard!" I said. "Where in the hell did you get that pistol?"

"Took it off'n a dead SS guy back at Budinger Wald," the sullen Packard replied.

I saw Rohan across the trail and ran over to him in a crouch. I told him we had a wounded Kraut machine gunner, maybe dead, but none of us had been hit. Then I asked him what we should do with the prisoner.

"Just leave him right there, Joy," Johnny Rohan said, "and keep going with your squad. There's another roadblock up ahead. The Second Platoon is coming up right behind you, and they'll take care of the Kraut."

So we took the wounded German's machine gun and ammo belt, pitched it out onto the trail behind us, and went on. Shortly another burst of fire came from across the road. There was an answering burst from several rifles and a BAR, and we heard a German voice cry, "*Kamerad! Kamerad!*" From the tree where I crouched down I could see across the road and could make out a German standing up with his hands raised. Then I saw "tough guy" Wilson stand up, point to someone on the ground next to him, and heard him shout, "*Kamerad*, my ass, there's my *Kamerad* on the ground, an' you shot him. I'll *Kamerad* you, ya Kraut bastard!"

With that, Wilson struck the frightened German a blow in the face, knocking him down. Then he picked the prisoner up and was about to strike him again when another burst of fire caused him and the German both to throw themselves to the ground. It was not until later that night that we learned who had been wounded before Wilson put on his stupid show. One of the men was Sergeant Outhouse, whom I did not know, and the other was a replacement in Bailey's squad named Foster.

We had not seen hide nor hair of our platoon leader, Lieutenant Tyler, until the firing died down. But now he came running from the road and through the woods to where we lay and gasped, "Sergeant Joy, the captain wants you to take two men back to that first roadblock and get your mortar off the jeep. Set it up and give them some fire support up there at that second roadblock."

I looked at the scared lieutenant and wanted to say something snotty to him. Instead I said okay, but I didn't bother to say "sir." I told Vincent and Packard to stay put while Decker, Hatley, and I went back to get our mortar. We moved in a crouch, back through the trees, and suddenly one of the 2d Platoon's rifleman raised up and said in a hoarse whisper, "Christ sake, guys, ya better get down and crawl, an' don't make so much noise or ya'll bring some more fire in here on us. We already got two guys killed! Where is that Kraut machine gunner y'all claimed to have wounded? We never came acrost him."

"You should have come across him just back there less than twenty yards," I said, pointing. "Where did your guys get killed?"

"You'll see 'em right back there where we left 'em, Mac," he said. "In that little clearing."

Sure enough, a few minutes later, as we dropped down and began to crawl back along that narrow trail, we came across two dead GIs. It was not until later that we learned they were 2d Platoon riflemen named Campbell and Hill. And then we came to the bloody spot where we had left the wounded German machine gunner. But he was nowhere to be seen! That was, and is to this day, a spooky mystery to me. Whether some of the German's friends had come out of the thick woods and dragged him away just after we left, we never knew. But that is what I, for one, suspect happened.

The three of us looked at each other, speechless, then looked at several thick clumps of trees on a slight rise to the right of the trail. We swung our rifles this way and that, and finally Decker said, "Jesus, where'd that Kraut go? Let's get out of here, quick!"

We crawled a few more yards as fast as we could, to where the trail cut left toward the road, and then we could make out some American helmets behind a log. I recognized the face of our burly battalion commander, Lieutenant Colonel Gettys, and saw two GIs hunkered down next to him, manning a tripod-mounted water-cooled machine gun. I stood up, waved, and spotted our supply sergeant's jeep and trailer parked under some trees a few yards farther on. I was now wearing the three stripes of a buck sergeant on my sleeves, and I remember feeling extremely nervous and self-conscious when Gettys beckoned me to come over to him.

"How bad is it up there, son?" he asked.

"Bad, sir," I stammered. "Roadblock. Two killed and several wounded, I think. They need some mortar fire, sir, and sent us back to get our mortar off the jeep."

"Okay, son. Better get cracking. Do you know the range?"

The honest answer to that question would have been "No, sir." But I didn't dare admit that I had no idea, so I just gulped and nodded "Yes, sir." Then I told Decker and Hatley to run to the jeep, quick, and fetch our mortar and a dozen rounds of ammo while I picked a good spot to set it up.

You don't just set a mortar up anywhere, especially if there are trees overhead; you need a clear opening to avoid having your mortar shells hit a limb or a branch and detonate just after the round leaves the tube. And so, with Gettys watching, I strode out from under the trees to a ditch alongside the road and found an open spot ten or fifteen yards in front of the log breastwork behind which he and the two GIs manning the machine gun were crouched. But now came my moment of truth. *Joy, you stupid jerk*, I said to myself. *What in hell is the range up to that roadblock? You should have paced it off when we came back up the trail through the woods!*

LTC GETTYS WATCHES ME PREPARE TO FIRE MORTAR

All I had to go by was the brown top of a sort of cliff I could see down the road, and I remembered that the roadblock—where Wilson had knocked down the German prisoner—was a few dozen yards just this side of that cliff. I don't know how long I looked at that cliff, trying to estimate its distance from where I stood, but there was no time to waste. I could hear sporadic rifle shots that I knew were M1s, and the short answering *brrrp-brrrp* of a German machine gun. So I made a guess: *Gotta be about eight hundred yards,* I said to myself.

As I stood there, Hatley came running up with the mortar base plate, followed by Decker, who carried the tube with its folded bipod legs and the bubble sight. Each of them also carried an ammo vest with six rounds. I could see that Decker was quite nervous. I had never been much impressed with his performance as gunner in setting up the mortar quickly and getting the bubbles in the sight leveled, so I impatiently grabbed the tube, said I would set it up, and told him to help Hatley get the rounds ready. In less than a minute I had the bubbles leveled and the vertical hair of the sight lined up on the center of the cliff. I took out my range card and told Decker, "Charge two."

But before Decker had removed two booster-charge wafers from the round he held in his hand, I had a change of heart. To be safe, I decided to set the range at 850 yards instead of 800. "Hold it, Glen; make that charge three," I said, and I cranked the tube elevation down one turn, to match the setting my range card gave for a range of 850 yards. I watched Decker strip just one wafer off the round and said, "Okay, fire one." I ducked my head to avoid the blast, and we waited.

Ten or so seconds later we heard the distant *crrump* of the shell exploding, and in another ten seconds I heard Gettys shout, "Right on target, son! Got Captain Neal on the radio and he says, fire for effect! Three rounds!" So we fired three more rounds.

As we waited for more orders, two H Company jeeps came roaring up. Several GIs piled out and unloaded two of their heavy 81mm mortars. As they set their big tubes up a few paces behind our position, their sergeant strode over and asked me what range we had used. I told him, but I remember little else of what happened then. I know only that the 81s fired several rounds, including white phosphorus, a particularly vicious type of smoke shell that burned the skin and clothes of anyone who got some of it on him. A few salvos of our artillery also came swishing overhead. Then, before we put our own mortar back on the jeep, Gettys congratulated me, said the Germans had surrendered, and told us we were to go on down the road to rejoin our company.

We hiked back along that dirt road, met up with our company, and soon were sweeping the woods on either side of the road leading to the next town. Rohan congratulated me, and I gulped when he said, "Joy, your very first round was a direct hit on that Kraut position, not thirty yards beyond where they had us pinned down." Needless to say, I did *not* tell him how I had changed the range at the last minute. Had I fired that first round at eight hundred yards it might well have landed right on Rohan and the others who were pinned down at that roadblock.

A short time later we came across an abandoned farmhouse, and in an attached shed we found several large glass jars containing what turned out to be strawberry jam. We laughed like maniacs as we hiked through those woods eating strawberry jam. We must have looked ludicrous—combat infantrymen skir-

A LUDICROUS SCENE—SPOONING JAM IN THE WOODS

mishing through that forest, faces and mouths smeared red, each with a rifle in one hand and the other hand using a mess kit spoon to gobble down that delicious jam from a big glass jar hanging with its wire handle hooked over our left arm.

We finally reached a small village in which we bedded down for the night in a brewery.

CHAPTER 20

THE DANUBE WASN'T BLUE

Saturday, April 21, through Monday, April 30, 1945

On the morning of our forty-third day in combat—Saturday, April 21—G Company attacked down a secondary highway a few miles northwest of a town called Sulzbach-Rosenburg. We did not know it then, but we were part of a wing of Patton's Third Army that Eisenhower had ordered to advance southeast along the southern border of Czechoslovakia, cross the Danube River, and proceed on east to meet the Russians coming west from Vienna.

The following paragraphs—excerpts taken from our 71st Division history book—explain the plan:

> The [XX] Corps plan called for an attack southeast with the 65th Infantry Division on the right, the 71st Infantry Division on the left, and the 80th Infantry and 13th Armored Divisions in reserve prepared to pass through on Corps order.
>
> The new division zone of operation was initially very

broad, and then narrowed down in two places. The terrain was rough, cut by many corridors, heavily wooded areas, and inhabited localities.

The division plan of attack called for initial commitment with all three regiments abreast. As the zone narrowed one regiment was to be pinched out and go into reserve. The demand for speed of movement, plus the distances and wide area to be covered, necessitated maneuver that would periodically relieve each regiment in turn.

The beginning battle formation found the 14th Combat Team on the left, the 5th Combat Team in the center, and the 66th Combat Team on the right. The 5th Infantry, operating in the center of the zone, and hindered more by a poor road net and terrain conditions than by enemy action, discovered a good four-lane military highway not appearing on the map. This road ran to Sulzbach, located in the original zone of the 14th Infantry Combat Team. When it became apparent that the 14th Infantry would be unable to accomplish the mission of seizing Sulzbach according to the time schedule, the 5th Infantry was authorized to cross over into the zone of the 14th Infantry and capture the town. By shuttling the troops forward using Antitank Company, Cannon Company, and organic vehicles, the 5th Infantry had advanced some seventeen miles forward on the 21st of April. Other elements of the 5th Infantry executed an encircling movement to the west and south to take the town of Rosenburg, thereby blocking the escape of enemy troops from Sulzbach.

On April 21, following an uneventful morning, during which G Company advanced in two columns along a road that ran along the side of a low ridge, we took a short lunch break in a clearing. We were covering the left flank of E Company as it attacked along the top of the ridge. While we ate our cold C rations, we heard the muffled sounds of rifles and automatic weapons, answered from time to time by the *brrrp-brrrp* of German Schmeisser machine pistols. In the narrow little valley down to our left rear, we could see the smoke from a burning town that was being attacked by our 1st Battalion and a platoon of five tanks.

Not long after the order came for us to move out, with my assault squad on the left, three or four scattered shots were fired at us from another low ridge across the valley, beyond the burning town. I was sure I had seen the muzzle flashes from a clump of bushes on that distant ridge—maybe three hundred or four hundred yards across the valley, so I ran forward to the edge of the trees to find a better place from which to scan the bushes with my binoculars.

Hatley was carrying our BAR that day; the five of us usually took turns carrying that twenty-pound weapon. I said to him, "C'mon, Waitus. I think I got 'em spotted. Here's your chance to use the BAR."

"Ah don't see nuttin'," he replied as we squatted down. I raised my binoculars again.

"Well, I sure as hell did," I said as I lowered the glasses and clicked off my M1's safety. "Watch those bushes over there. I'm gonna fire a couple tracer rounds to show you where I think they are. Looks like about three hundred or three hundred fifty yards. Unfold your bipod and fire a full clip. That BAR is more accurate at that range than my M1."

With that I stretched out flat in the approved prone position, took aim, and fired two tracer rounds at that clump of bushes. Before Hatley could get set up to fire the BAR, old Top came running over from the rear, where he usually marched with the company headquarters section. He glared at me and gasped, "Who gave ya the order to fire, Sergeant Joy? What ya shootin' at?"

"Kraut sharpshooters, Top," I said. "In those bushes over there. See?"

But we both looked with our binoculars and saw nothing. By

now the rest of my squad had come up beside us to look. Packard snickered and said to no one in particular, "*Bet he didn't see nothin'. Just showin' off.*"

Well, if Packard had not already gotten himself on my shit list, he sure was on it now. I just ignored him. First Sergeant Anderson walked back into the trees, shaking his head. Then the order was passed to move on along the ridge. In another half hour or so we started down toward a gently sloping open field with a few houses on our right, and a railroad angling in parallel to our route of advance. Several old women stood by the dirt road in front of the houses, and we could see that they were very frightened.

The gray-headed old women all had wrinkled brown faces, wore kerchiefs and drab clothes, and as we marched past them they were wringing their hands on their aprons. Two or three opened their mouths, showing bad teeth, trying to smile, and kept repeating, over and over again, "Wir sind nicht Nazis!— nicht Nazis!—nicht Nazis!"

This litany, which we knew meant "We are not Nazis," was repeated in a sort of singsong, off-key whine. It irritated us, and several of us laughed and retorted, "Ja, ja, du bist Nazis, all of you!—Nazis!—Nazis!"

Those poor, harmless old women! I remember some of them had tear-stained cheeks, and today I am ashamed as I remember that little episode. But it tells something of our own fear and anger at the entire German people for what we had been through and what still lay ahead.

On down that gentle slope we marched, following the railroad now, with Captain Neal up ahead of the column, leading the way. Suddenly we saw Neal stop and raise his hand to signal a halt. Then we could see he was speaking on his walkie-talkie. And shortly the word was passed back along the line, "Easy Company is chasing a whole bunch of Krauts our way! Everybody up to the top of that ridge on the right! On the double!"

One Sherman medium tank was following our column, and

when this order came, the tank cut sharply right to crawl up the ridge toward a clump of trees. As our long column of infantry formed a skirmish line and started up toward the top of that ridge to the left of the trees where the tank was headed, there was a sudden *whoosh-crraaack* over to my left.

I looked up and was startled to see the gray-black smoke of an artillery air burst. The *whoosh-crraaack* had sounded behind us. I turned to look back at the other ridge across the valley and I immediately spotted a flash from what I recognized as a German tank on the skyline of that ridge, perhaps half a mile away—*behind* us!

There was a second *whoosh-crraaack,* this one louder as a closer air burst went off over the heads of the now running line of skirmishers on my left. Then a third air burst went off—but this one was way over to my right, just above the Sherman tank. Then I knew that this damn tank of ours was drawing the fire. It took less than a minute for that Sherman to back down the slope and disappear behind one of the houses where we had seen the old women.

After the third shell had burst over the tank, I thought it best to run to my left, to gain the protection of some distant trees in that direction. But then there were more air bursts, and I realized that the German gunner was traversing his shots back to the left again, aiming at the line of running infantrymen. I followed my squad toward the clump of trees to which our tank had been headed. It was during that run that I felt, rather than heard, a concussion from overhead, and I looked up to see the dissipating smoke of an air burst no more than ten or fifteen feet above my head!

By the time I joined my squad in the relative safety of those trees, the shelling had stopped. But I began to shake when one of them said, "Jesus Christ, Joy, are ya okay? I saw that last one go off right over your head! And look out there! Some of those guys who were behind ya got hit!"

A CLOSE SHAVE—GERMAN TANK SHELL AIRBURST

All I could do was nod. Then we heard the cry "Medic!," and when I looked back over that open slope I saw that two men were down. As near as we could guess, pieces of shrapnel from that tank shell had sprayed downward in a wide cone, missing me entirely but wounding two GIs who must have been running at least fifty yards behind me. I never found out who or how badly wounded they were. Nor did I realize until some time later that I couldn't hear very well with my left ear. I didn't learn until after the war that I had lost 50 percent of the hearing in my ear as a result.

It took a while for G Company to get reorganized. We never did see any of the enemy troops that E Company was supposed to be chasing in our direction. In any case, later that afternoon it began to rain, and we soon reached another woods that needed to be swept. Something got messed up with our captain's map reading and navigation before dark. After we had swept one large patch of woods we formed a column on a very muddy trail, and stopped several times as we hiked along.

We could see Neal and other officers ahead of us, looking at a folded map in the rain, consulting their compasses, and talking on the radio. After the third or fourth halt, Platoon Sergeant Cree went forward to see what was going on. When he returned he said, "Wrong woods. We've gone almost in a complete circle."

After that snafu we marched for several more miles in the rain and mud, and finally we came to a small village of four or five farmhouses, deep in a forest. We spent a scary night in that village. Our mortar section shared a large barn—empty except for a rickety table and a few old chairs—with a squad from one of our rifle platoons. We had a sound-powered telephone in the barn, courtesy of one of the communications section's wiremen. It got very cold that night, so Nero, the rifle platoon sergeant, allowed us to build a small fire in an open space on the dirt floor of the barn. That turned out to be a rather stupid and dangerous thing to do, but it reminded me of the warehouse back in Fulda, where I had agreed to have a small fire built so we could keep warm. In this case, however, the old barn was not very lightproof, and it's a wonder we didn't get into more trouble than we did.

We had guards posted at each of the four corners of the barn, and several of the NCOs, myself included, were assigned phone guard duty, two hours at a stretch. I happened to be awake, sitting on a rickety chair by the fire, listening as whoever it was who manned our phone whispered his responses to someone at company headquarters calling for a check. Suddenly there was a frightening burst of German machine-gun fire, and several rounds of tracer bullets went zinging through the barn's walls!

"Douse the fire, douse the fire!" someone rasped. As we hurriedly put the fire out we heard the phone man whispering, "What? What? A full-scale counterattack?"

The night of April 21–22 ended with no counterattack worthy of the name, but the next morning we learned that two of our riflemen were wounded by a Kraut patrol, and then we later learned that one GI from E Company had been killed by the same patrol.

The next morning, April 22, while we were out sweeping the woods in the rain, someone had brought the dead E Company soldier's body into our barn and left it face up on the table. When we returned just before noon, there it was. And someone said that the GI had been on guard in a farmhouse, sitting at a dark window, and had been shot when he used a match or a lighter to light his cigarette. Why they left him in our barn I never knew. But hearing how he had been shot was sobering.

As I think back on that noontime in the barn, with several of us standing around that dead stranger on the table, now and then sneaking a look at his face or trying to guess where he had been hit, I wonder about something. Was it just morbid curiosity that drew some of us to want to remain close to that stranger for a bit—even to the point of wanting to reach out and touch that dread, mysterious corpse? Or was it some sort of defensive, macholike mechanism that prevented us from leaving? And why did no one suggest that we take his body outside? Was it a way of saying to our buddies, "Hey, Mac, I can take this as long as you can—I am a combat infantryman and have grown a very thick skin where death is concerned?" All I can say now is that I must have been trying very hard not to care, or show that I cared. But inside I cared very much.

I might better understand the desire to touch if it had been a friend, like Sergeant Alfred Feltman or Private Jesus Lozano. And I could understand the need to hover around had it been a beloved relative in a casket, at a funeral. But a complete stranger?

No one objected when one young rifleman, who said he could use a new web belt, as his own was frayed, decided to roll

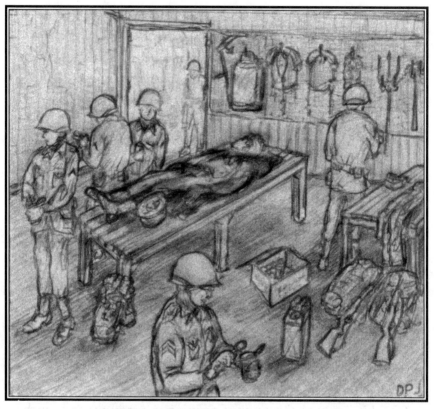

LUNCH IN A BARN WITH A DEAD GI ON THE TABLE

the corpse on its side and take the web belt from his bloody pants. All of us must have been thinking the same thing: *It's too damn cold and wet outside, and we're hungry. So, by God, we'll eat our C ration lunch right here.* And that we did.

It is a curious fact that back then, had the corpse been a German, I doubt if I would have given its presence a second thought, except maybe to insist that the offensive enemy intruder be dumped outside—out of sight and mind—so we could enjoy our lunch.

Later in the afternoon, after we had left our barn and marched up a winding road to a sort of plateau overlooking the town of

Rosenburg, we took a break, and some of us wandered over to inspect a platoon of half-tracks on which 76mm antitank guns were mounted.

Suddenly the platoon's lieutenant, who had been scanning the town and hills beyond with his binoculars, spotted a German tank slowly poking its nose out from behind some houses on a ridge across the way. The range to that tank must have been almost a mile. In the next minute or two we had a ringside seat as one of the half-tracks pivoted a bit to bring its gun to bear; then its crew fired two quick rounds in succession. The tank blew up, and we cheered. Who knows but that it may have been the same tank that nearly got me with an air burst the day before.

The order to move out came shortly after that, and we hiked down a switchback road into Rosenburg, which had white flags flying everywhere. A few German troops in the city surrendered without a fight.

After dark, the last notable event of the day took place. We came upon a log roadblock between trees bordering the entrance to a small village. The roadblock was readily removed, and a sign beyond it identified the village as Fuchstein. By then I knew enough German to explain to the others that the German word *Fuchs* was pronounced "Foox" and means "fox." But that didn't stop several wags from calling the little town Fuckstein.

Our mortar section was bringing up the rear of G Company's column that night, and just as we passed the roadblock, a bell began to ring from a small church a short distance up a dark path to our left. Word was quickly passed back down the line to us, "Someone go stop that damn bell!"

Before Rohan or I could give the order, Packard, Hatley, and Vincent took off up that dark path toward the church. I ran after them, and as I came up to the open door, the bell stopped ringing. I saw Packard holding his big captured German revolver, standing over an old sexton, who was sitting on the floor next to the dangling bell rope, holding his bleeding head.

"Damn it, Packard," I called, "did you have to hit that old guy with your pistol?"

"Jus' tapped him once on the head when he wouldn't quit a-pullin' on that rope," Packard answered grumpily. I told him and Hatley to take the old man down to the street and ask Rohan what to do with him.

A few minutes later we were again bringing up the rear of the company as it advanced in two columns down the dark street. Our mortar section's job was to guard prisoners sent back from the leading patrols, and soon we had about thirty of them to frisk and put in the line of march. Most of them were sick or slightly wounded. Under interrogation later that night, several of them said that about fifty of their buddies had left the town not an hour before we arrived.

We spent the night in one of the houses in Fuchstein. Thus ended our forty-fourth day in combat.

The next day, Monday, April 23, was a red-letter day in terms of the number of prisoners we took. In my little notebook I wrote: "We bypass Amberg, go to the south of it, 90 prisoners from 1 house! Hike all day—final tabulation—200 prisoners 1 day. G Company is first into Schwandorf, riding 'H' Company jeeps. Good billet."

We turned the prisoners over to First Sergeant Anderson and a group of his headquarters men who were bringing up the rear. Then my squad and I rode for about another ten miles as passengers in two H Company jeeps. We bypassed Amberg, drove south down a paved road, leading the way for the entire 2d Battalion, and were the first troops to enter the town of Schwandorf.

That night, as we relaxed in the house we had taken over as a billet, someone told a story of another atrocity involving a prisoner. There was never any proof of this, but the story was that First Sergeant Anderson had volunteered that morning to escort a particularly obnoxious German officer back through the woods, to where the battalion intelligence section was supposed to have a POW interrogation center. But Anderson, it was said, had returned less than five minutes later, alone, and claimed that the German officer had tried to escape. So he shot him.

My notebook entry for the next day, Tuesday, April 24, was quite short and reads as follows: "Password {Valentines-Day}. Shuttled to Maxhutte. Eat more chicken. Good billet."

We must have reached Maxhutte before noon. I had time to write a three-page letter home. In one paragraph I said,

> *Our bedrolls didn't get to us (my stationery is in mine) so I am using this typewriter paper—My razor, soap, etc. is in my roll & therefore isn't with me at present. I've got a week's growth of beard, with dirt picked up along the 50 miles or so we've walked, mixed in. You sure wouldn't allow me in the house the way I am now, Mother.*

My beard has never been fast-growing or heavy, and in those days I could go for two days without shaving, yet no one could notice much red stubble to speak of. And so, after I had a full week's growth, I became somewhat proud as I examined my beard in a German mirror every chance I got.

Wednesday, April 25, and the predawn hours of Thursday, April 26, were long, long hours of hard, bone-wearying marching followed by riding on trucks, then marching some more. We were headed south toward the fabled Danube River. I estimate that the total distance we traveled that day and night was nearly thirty miles, at least half of it on foot. Here are a few excerpts from my 71st Division history book that tell some of the story of the plans and movements of which we were a part:

By this time, from a study of captured documents and interrogation of prisoners of war, it was definitely established that the enemy was fighting a delaying action in an effort to gain time to rally their forces on the Danube in the hope of making a determined stand there. Instructions were received from Corps to accelerate the drive of the Division and to bypass small pockets of enemy encountered as they would be cared for by Corps reserve. The Division SOP [Standing Operation Procedure] of carefully searching all the houses was abandoned on the basis of these instructions. Units of the Division utilized every possible means of transportation to speed the attack.

In the railway yards of the captured city [of Schwandorf] searching GIs found a train of locked boxcars. Breaking the cars open the Yanks released a load of Russian and Polish prisoners. Abandoned by their guards, and without food or water for several days, many had already died, while the majority of those still alive came from . . . chambers of torture in an emaciated and hysterical condition, nearer to the land of the dead than that of the living.

While engaged in difficult and wide-sweeping operations, and still many miles from the north bank of the Danube, an order was received from the XX Corps to cross the Danube River the night of April 25–26. The 5th Infantry, hampered by a poor road net, reached the river shortly after midnight, while the 66th Infantry was fighting in the city of Regensburg on the north side of the Danube. The Division plan of attack called for an assault on a broad front with simultaneous river crossings by the 5th and 14th Infantries. Division Artillery had moved into position to cover the crossings, and the 1139th Engineer Combat Group was ready to move to either crossing site as the situation developed. The time of the attack was set at 2:00 a.m, April 26.

However, it became apparent that troops and materiel would not be in position for the assault crossing at the specified time. Pockets of by-passed enemy units blocked the roads delaying the passage of assault boats and materiels. Organization of the regiments for the crossing was of necessity being carried on after dark. . . . The attacking hour was delayed until 4:00 a.m.

Doughs of the 5th Infantry slid down the bank at the foot of the main street of a little town on the north bank of the Danube, and in the darkness clambered into assault boats, placed their weapons on the bottoms, and grasped the paddles in readiness for the dash to the opposite bank. Early waves made the crossing unopposed, quickly overran close up defense positions, then penetrated toward the rear before the enemy could react. Later crossings were made under fire, but the initial tactical surprise had been so complete that all elements were able to establish contact on the south bank.

My journal notes for that approach to, and crossing of, the Danube River on Wednesday and Thursday, April 25 and 26, were quite brief. This tells me that I had little time to sit down and record what happened.

On Wednesday we made a long, tiring road march from the town of Maxhutte to a small riverside village a few miles east of Regensburg. I remember vividly how miserable it was to be wakened after fewer than two hours' sleep and told to load up quickly and head down the street to the river, where some engineers were waiting in the dark to help load us into the boats. I was terribly afraid of drowning, as I was a poor swimmer. There were no life belts in our boat, and the Danube must have been at least half a mile wide where we crossed. I pulled fast and hard on those oars, turning my head frequently to see how far we had to go to reach the south bank. Why those boats had no outboard motors I do not know.

The first German mortars and a few rounds of flat-trajectory 88mm shells began to hit just as we climbed out of our boat and started up the muddy bank. I pitied the engineers of our 271st Engineer Combat Battalion, who had to stay there at the river crossing under fire. Some of them had already begun to build a pontoon bridge over to the south bank, not far from where our boats were launched. We knew how urgent this was, because until that bridge was ready, we had no tank support, not even as much as one jeep, on the south side of the river.

ROW, ROW YOUR BOAT—CROSSING THE DANUBE RIVER

There was no town at the river's edge where we landed—just a few trees. Beyond the trees a wide, flat field stretched southward about a mile to two or three distant villages. It was now growing light enough for us to see several church steeples on the horizon, and if we could see those steeples, what a view any German observers must have had as G Company got itself organized and advanced across that field in a broad skirmish line.

The long, wide field was dry and dusty, with patches of short brown grass here and there. We were sweating as we trudged across that field with our heavy loads. Captain Neal had wisely decided that we might need some mortar fire support before our own tanks and artillery could get across the river that morning. As a result, our mortar section of three squads, carrying our three mortars and led by Johnny Rohan, marched slightly behind the line of skirmishers.

We had gone no more than two hundred or three hundred yards when I saw many little dirt puffs rise close ahead, to my left and right. Then I heard several whispering *pssst-pssst* sounds at my feet, saw two riflemen ahead fall, and knew immediately that the puffs were spent bullets from one or more enemy machine guns firing at extreme range.

Seconds later the order came back from Captain Neal: Lay some mortar fire on the nearest town. A minute later, under Rohan's direction, all three mortars were set up, and each tube fired three or four rounds. That was the only time during combat that all three of our mortars fired in unison. In fact, it was the last time that G Company's "light artillery" fired its mortars in combat.

A day or two before we crossed the Danube, two short little Moroccan GIs dressed in French Army uniforms hooked up with us, saying in their fractured English that they were lost. Some of us suspected that they had deserted from whatever French unit they had been with, but since they were willing to act as scouts for one of our rifle platoons in exchange for food, that is where they were assigned.

At about noontime we arrived at the first town, and the two little Moroccans led the way as advance scouts for the rifle platoon ahead of us. We heard shots, and as we entered the village, we came across the bodies of two Germans just outside the doorway of a building. One of the riflemen nearby told us that the Germans had come out of the building with their hands up but that the Moroccans had shot them down anyway. This story seems to confirm what I had always heard about Moroccans, including what Hemingway wrote about them in his Spanish Civil War masterpiece *For Whom the Bell Tolls*—that Moroccans seldom took prisoners.

As we approached the next town, we were suddenly attacked by our *own* P-51 fighters! By this time a bridge had been built and one of our company jeeps had caught up with us, driven by our supply section's "armorer-articifer." We were by then advancing in column, down a road toward this next town, and there was a barbed-wire fence on my left. We heard the snarling of many high-powered aircraft engines coming from behind us, and when I looked back, there were several red-nosed Mustang P-51s headed south toward us. We cheered them on, but suddenly the lead pilot flipped over and began a screaming dive on our column!

The red nose of that P-51 pointing straight down at us was a terrifying sight to behold. A split second after I heard its six .50-caliber machine guns begin to chatter, I leaped over the barbed-wire fence bordering the road on my left, tearing my pants leg and gashing my calf in the process. We were lucky that only one man in the column behind us was slightly wounded before the pilot realized his error and pulled up.

The gash in my leg was not deep, and I used my first-aid kit to bandage it. Someone told me that the wound qualified me for the Purple Heart, but I doubted that, inasmuch as it wasn't a bullet wound and I didn't need the attention of a medic.

When the company re-formed on the road, one of our officers ran red-faced back to the jeep that had stopped at the rear of the column, and we could see him talking angrily with our "armorer-articifer"—the jeep's driver. This was an older man who was supposed to have immediately stopped when he heard

"HEY, MUSTANG THROTTLE JOCKIES, WE'RE FRIENDS!"

the planes, and to have displayed a colored panel that identified us as friendly. He had stopped, all right, but had crawled under his jeep in a panic and forgotten about displaying the panel.

There is an interesting footnote to this little episode. In 1949, when I was in my senior year back at the University of Colorado studying aeronautical engineering, one of my fellow students was a guy who had been a major in the U.S. Army Air Force. It turns out that he had flown P-51s with the Ninth Tactical Air Force, which had supported our armies in Europe. When I told him about how we were strafed by P-51s the day we crossed the Danube, he said, "Hell, Dean, that could have been me. We flew a mission down across the Danube the day it was crossed. But ya know, one hill looks like another up there, and unless you guys had yer panels out, how were we supposed ta know ya weren't Krauts?"

On the morning of April 27 we marched on foot for a while, but that afternoon we rode trucks in a convoy headed east on the highway toward the town of Straubing. At about dusk we came to a village named Pfatter, and were greeted there by sporadic enemy artillery fire. Our trucks dropped us off at the edge of the village and headed back to the west. G Company's mortar section was billeted that night on the ground floor of a small hotel, and we posted two guards in the semisheltered entrance doorway, across the street from the company CP, behind which was a large barn.

Someone from my squad noticed a shuttered meat market next door to the hotel, and he and others from the mortar section smashed open the door and found what looked like a fresh side of beef. They brought the bloody chunk of meat back to the hotel, carved it up, and that night we ate steak. It turned out to be horsemeat, not beef, but it tasted good to me.

Waitus Hatley found two old guitars in that hotel. After listening to him play and sing several Alabama-style folk tunes I had never heard before, I asked him to show me how to finger some of the chords. That was my introduction to the guitar and marked the beginning of my love for folk music.

That was a welcome respite from the war, but as we sat there in the relative safety of that little ground-floor hotel lobby, strumming those guitars, now and then a German artillery shell exploded somewhere down the street. One shell hit very close, and whoever was on guard at the entrance ducked back inside to tell us that the barn behind the company CP had been set on fire. There was no wind, the fire did not spread, and by the time I took my turn on guard outside, it had gone out.

Sometime after the war ended one of my former ASTP

GUITAR PLAYERS IN A SMALL HOTEL NEAR THE DANUBE

friends told me a surprising story. He said that the next day—
Saturday, April 28—his company had sent him with a patrol into
some woods south of Pfatter and there, by a farmhouse, they
had came across a German 75mm howitzer. They next came
across several youngsters in the uniform of the Hitler Jugend
(Hitler Youth). The oldest boy was no more than sixteen, but he
and the others admitted that they had been left behind, and had
been the gun crew that fired on our village the night before.

Over the next several days, as we moved fast toward Austria
and our meeting with the Russians, we captured many hundreds
of prisoners, and were surprised that so many of them were
teenagers who had hardly begun to shave.

On April 28, our tank support finally arrived, and we really began to roll. Here is an extract from our division history that tells some of the story:

> Two of the most famous rivers of continental Europe now lay behind the 71st Division. The Rhine and the Danube, source of lyrical outpourings by scores of romanticists in the days of peace, had become conversational fixtures among the realists of the 71st.
>
> Ahead of the Division stretched the broad valley of the mighty Danube, a gently rolling area broken at intervals by the many tributaries of the Danube, including the major rivers, Isar, Inn, and the Enns, and bounded on the south by the jagged, snow-capped spires of the Alps.
>
> The plan of battle called for continued attack in a southeastern direction with the 71st Infantry the center prong of a three division front. Serving as a spearhead was the 13th Armored Division, scheduled to drive southeast, then to swing directly south across the Corps front and disorganize enemy resistance within the zone of operation.
>
> Within the Division zone, the 5th Infantry was to operate on the left flank, the 66th Infantry on the right flank, and the 14th Infantry initially in reserve, was to be committed as the zone broadened. The 71st Cavalry Recon Troop covered the north flank, along the shore of the Danube.

Here is what I recorded in my little notebook for that April 28: "Password {Dorothy-Lamour}. Wake up in morning to hear our welcome tanks pass through town. Our division is the 'pivot' of the Corps, on the Danube, behind 3 arm'd Divisions, out to meet the Russians. Tanks are 30 miles out ahead before afternoon! We walk to Greisau, Schonach, Atting, screen civilians in all 3 towns, billet in the last. Rain all afternoon."

That Saturday was officially our fiftieth day in combat. So far we had heard at least some shots fired at us every day, but it can be argued that we were not in much danger on some of those days.

In fact, I must admit that the surviving combat infantry veterans from divisions such as the 1st Infantry (known as Big Red One), or the 3rd or 29th or 36th or 45th—to name just a few that saw many more months of hard combat than we did—might well think that the 71st had a picnic, relatively speaking. All I can say to those vets is, *Gents, I have read about what most of you went through, and what we saw of combat can't hold a candle to your experiences, but our total of sixty days on the line were more than enough for me.*

And so April 1945 came to an end. Here is what our Division history has to say about our operations during the last three days of that month:

> The Isar River presented the first barrier in the path of the advancing 71st Infantry Division. The drive southeast began on April 28. During the day the Third Battalion, 5th Infantry, motorized, sped to the city of Straubing which had been passed by the armor. Without opposition the city was captured and 1900 prisoners seized.
>
> To the 14th and 66th Infantries fell the task of forcing bridgeheads on the Isar. The 5th Infantry was to pass to the center of the zone beyond the Isar after using the sites established by her two sister regiments.
>
> During the afternoon of April 30, under cover of a barrage and smoke, heavy machine guns were moved into positions along the [Isar] river near where the crossing was to be forced. Late in the day a heavy smoke screen was laid over enemy positions and the assault began.
>
> The bridgeheads eliminating the first water obstacle in the Division path had been established. From this shallow foothold

on the east side of the Isar the attack was continued, three regiments abreast against light and scattered enemy resistance.

All I can remember about our approach to the Isar is that it
was another long hike of perhaps ten miles down the highway
from Straubing to our crossing site, which was just across the river
from a town called Landau. We didn't know that after the Isar we
still had two major rivers to cross—the Inn and the Enns—before
the war ended.

We were the far right wing of Patton's Third Army, and
Patch's Seventh Army was on our right flank headed for Munich
and points south in Bavaria. We knew that the French First Army
was farther south, advancing east from the Black Forest along
Germany's southern border with Switzerland. We also knew
that the American Fifth Army was moving north from Italy into
the Austrian and Bavaria Alps, headed for a junction with the
Seventh Army at the famous Brenner Pass. But our greatest fear
was that some of Hitler's most faithful SS troops might try to escape south into the Alpine mountain regions that Eisenhower
had called the German National Redoubt. How long the ensuing
guerrilla war might last if that happened was anybody's guess.

But we had seen and crossed the fabled Danube, and although I saw no blood in those waters, that river was surely *not*
blue.

CHAPTER 21

THE LAST BATTLES

Tuesday, May 1, through Tuesday, May 8, 1945

The final eight days of my war as a combat infantryman passed rapidly. We traveled an estimated one hundred miles during that last week, at least half of that distance on foot. Every day we came under some fire from diehard German units—sometimes at long range, but more often at close quarters or in woods or villages.

The week began on Tuesday, May 1, with a long walk to the Isar River crossing at Landau. Unlike at the Danube, we didn't have to row ourselves across—the engineers ferried us across in boats powered by outboard motors.

We bypassed Landau, which had been taken earlier by our sister 66th Infantry Regiment, and on a small secondary road east of that place our three assault squads were placed in the lead. Suddenly Willie Burns, of Bailey's squad, gave a shout and ran up on top of the six-foot road embankment on our right, carrying his BAR. A few of us followed him up the bank, and I saw what looked like a long, low tent, and beyond the tent I caught a glimpse of a German officer kneeling by some kind of box.

Burns didn't even bother to kneel; he just stopped quickly, raised his BAR to his shoulder, and fired a quick burst of three or four rounds. As he fired, the German officer jerked, and we knew he was hit. But when he fell over, his hand pushed down on what turned out to be a detonation plunger. There was a tremendous concussion, and whatever had been under that tentlike covering went up in a blinding flash. We all fell flat as pieces of debris and parts of that German officer flew high into the air. Some of the debris came down through the smoke and landed near where we lay.

Apparently the suicidal German had blown up a small ammo dump, probably dynamite or TNT. It might have made

WILLIE BURNS SHOOTS A SUICIDAL SS OFFICER

more sense if he had waited until our column got closer, as the dump was only a few yards from the road. We figured that he didn't expect anyone like sharp-eyed Willie Burns to spot him at that distance—probably at least seventy or eighty yards. In any case, if he wanted to die, he got his wish. From pieces of his uniform it was determined that he was an SS captain or major.

Although we were told there were many SS troops in our path, we saw or heard no more action that day.

On Wednesday morning, May 2, we were trucked a few miles to the town of Pfarrkirchen, a small road junction on a pretty stream named the Rott. Spanish oranges were distributed to us in the central square of that little town. What pleasure I had, peeling and eating my orange, as I sat on a stone bridge railing

SPANISH ORANGES FOR LUNCH ON A PEACEFUL BRIDGE

with the sun warm on my back, and watched the shadows of trout in that fast-moving stream.

I almost dozed off on that bridge, dreaming of the many precious times I had had with my father on fishing trips in the Rocky Mountains of Colorado and Wyoming.

But that afternoon G Company was back at the grim business of war. We undertook what was probably the longest hike I ever made on foot in one day (and half a night). We were headed for the Inn River—the border between Germany and Austria. That hike was well over thirty miles, including a five-mile backtrack and round-trip that my unlucky squad had to make to bring up our mortar. Those extra ten miles constitute a story in themselves. To help explain the situation that led to this long road march, here is an excerpt from our division's history book:

> The 13th Armored Division, working ahead of the slower moving foot troops, had already reached the Inn. From that unit a report was received that all bridges across the river in the 71st Division's zone of advance had been destroyed. Division engineers, riding as observers in the grasshoppers [light observation aircraft] of the artillery, confirmed the report after a series of reconnaissance flights along the river.
>
> However, the scouting parties did find two large and unharmed dams which, it was believed, could be pressed into use as crossing sites, if they could be captured before the retreating Germans could destroy them. In the late afternoon of May 2 motorized battalions of the 5th and 66th Infantries moved ahead of the advancing Division forces with the mission of seizing and securing the dams.
>
> The Second Battalion of the 5th Infantry reached the river at Ering where a contact was made with enemy forces defending the dam. Operating in broad daylight, with a flanking force assaulting in boats, the Battalion fought its way across the dam and captured a demolition crew who had been ordered to de-

stroy the structure. The wires leading to the implaced demolitions were cut while the fighting for possession of the dam was in progress. By midnight of that day half the unit was in a perimeter defense on the south side of the river, while the remainder of the Battalion was in similar positions on the north side. One bridgehead for the crossing into Austria was now certain.

Although G Company walked most of the way to the Inn River, and although we were not part of the little flanking task force that crossed the river in assault boats, we were the second of two companies of our battalion to walk across the dam. First across was F Company.

En route to that crossing we took many prisoners, and once even shot rifles and BARs at a German light plane, but we failed to hit it.

The tankers of the 761st Tank Battalion I saw in action were very brave, but some of them were also really wild men when it came to shooting up the countryside with their 75mm guns.

Earlier on the afternoon of May 2, a platoon of 761st Battalion tanks was following along behind our advance scouts. Just as we were passing a large farmhouse and barn on a rise to the left of the dirt road, a wind began to blow, and large, ominous clouds overhead turned the sky dark with a threat of rain. One or two of the tank commanders decided for some reason to blast away at that farm. We had received no fire from the house or barn or the surrounding area, but maybe the tankers saw something we didn't.

The barn soon caught fire. The wind was blowing harder, and out through the open door of that burning barn dashed a beautiful black stallion, his mane flying. He jumped a corral fence and took off across the fields. An old woman, dressed all in black, her long, wide skirts flying, ran out from the house and tried vainly to catch that stallion. What a dramatic scene that was!

Later, when G Company trudged down the slope to the dam over the Inn River, watching F Company's rifle squads preparing

A BIG BLACK STALLION ESCAPES FROM A BURNING BARN

to start across, that same tank platoon was lined up on a ridge to our right, overlooking the river. Although we could see no targets or gun flashes from the town on the other side, those five tanks had a great time blasting away, shell after shell, until the town was covered with smoke and several of the nearest houses were turned into rubble.

We crossed the dam, following F Company, at about dusk that day, and were told that some of the demolition charges the Germans had set to blow up the dam were captured five hundred-pound U.S. Army Air Force bombs. We heard that F Company's advance party had cut the wires to these charges and captured the German demolition crew. But the charges were still in place, and

I was fearful as we crossed, thinking there might be backup wires that had not been found, and imagining that I would be blown sky high and end up dead in the river below.

G COMPANY CROSSES THE INN RIVER ON A DAM

It was growing dark and had begun to drizzle when we finally got across and passed through a platoon of F Company that had set up a defensive position around one of the first houses. Our column then turned right, and we walked a block or two down the main street toward the town center, which was lit up by the flames of a burning building. There we were brought to a halt as word was passed back, "Live wires down in the street."

In the town square we saw a large horse-drawn wagon, and one electrocuted horse, obviously dead, lying in the tangled harness. Another horse struggled to pull free. GIs and German civilians stood on the curb, but no one dared venture over to that wagon to help the horse because of the sparking live wires strewn all over the wet pavement.

Just as our mortar section was about to enter the house we were to occupy that night, Rohan came back from a meeting with Captain Neal, drew me aside, and gave me the bad news: "Neal says you and your squad gotta go back and get a mortar and some ammo. Leave your BAR and bazooka here, and he wants you to take along a wagonload of wounded civilians and a couple of prisoners to help push it."

I cursed under my breath, wondering why my squad and I always seemed to get the shit details, but I didn't raise any argument. The cart was just large enough to carry three wounded civilians. With two German boys pulling and the two German POWS pushing, we set off back down the street toward the dam.

Vincent, Packard, and I carried M1 rifles with fixed bayonets. The three of us brought up the rear to make sure the POWs didn't try to escape. Hatley and Decker had only their .45 Colt automatics, so I sent them on ahead. Their job was to help move barbed-wire coils, if necessary, so the cart could pass.

It took us three hours to make that round-trip over the dam and back to Ering. Some officer on the northeast bank told me to wait, to show the way for a ration detail from battalion headquarters. They were bringing backpacks loaded with C rations and cans of water to the part of the battalion that had crossed the river, because it had not yet received its daily rations allowance.

It must have been at about midnight—maybe later—when my miserably dog-tired 3d Mortar Squad finally got back to where we supposed our billet for the night was located. I was furious when we learned that the mortar section had been moved; no one seemed to know where. This time, when I finally came across our buddies asleep in a different house, and saw Johnny Rohan I really let him have it! So ended our fifty-fourth day in combat.

. . .

The next day, Friday, May 4, we were told that our regiment was no longer in reserve, and that the division now had the mission of moving fast to contact the Russians at the Enns River, some fifty miles east of the Inn.

After passing through Altheim, Ried, Haag-am-Hausruck, and several other Austrian "dorfs," we captured the town of Lambach. Before noon that day, Bailey and I were sent with our assault squads on a woodcutter's trail that led into a heavily wooded area to the right of the dirt road on which we had been marching. We were told to watch for one or more German tanks reported to be coming down that trail in our direction.

Bailey and one of his men lagged behind for some reason, so I was leading our little patrol. Before long we came to a fork in the trail, and I stopped because I was sure I heard the telltale rumble of a tank in the distance. With my little group were two antitank bazookas—one carried by Vincent, of my squad, and the other by the Boston Irish kid we called Shaky Hayes, who was a member of Bailey's squad.

Shortly, Bailey came up to me to inquire why we had stopped, and when I told him, he decided to take two of his men and a BAR into the woods bordering the right-hand trail, to make a brief reconnaissance. The other six men and I hunkered down behind a few bushes at the trail junction and prepared to engage the tank with our two bazookas. We heard that tank engine start up twice, and then we heard several distant American voices off in the woods shout *"Tank! Tank!"*

The World War II–vintage American 3.5-inch bazooka was simply a long metal tube open at both ends. It had a shoulder rest, trigger mechanism, and battery beneath the center of the tube, and a screen flashguard mounted to protect the gunner's face from hot little particles of rocket propellant when the bazooka fired. The rocket itself was 3.5 inches in diameter and about 18 inches long, with a shaped-charge warhead at the nose and a propelling rocket extending back to the tail, which had stabilizing fins and an electrical wire attached. After the assistant gunner loaded the rocket into the rear of the launcher, he had to pull out the coiled wire and attach its end to a little metal post sticking out of the battery compartment. The rocket would not fire unless this was all done properly. A good assistant gunner could do it in fifteen seconds or less.

After I made sure that Decker had properly loaded Vincent's bazooka, I looked over at Hayes and asked, "You know how to fire that thing, right, Shaky?" He shook his head and said, "Never was any good at it. Here, Sarge, you fire it, and I will load it for ya."

I set down my rifle, put the launcher on my shoulder, and said, "Load it quick now, Shaky. I can hear that damn tank coming!"

MY BAZOOKA TEAM HEARS A TANK APPROACHING

I should have known better than to tell Hayes to load the thing. He got the rocket in the tube okay, but he was all thumbs when it came to wrapping the end of the wire around the battery post. Finally, with me cursing and begging him to hurry, Decker crawled over and did the job. We waited and waited as the tank engine seemed to come nearer and nearer, and we all "sweat the big drop," as they say. But then the noise began to recede, and soon we could tell that the tank had turned around to leave.

Bailey and his two men returned to our position in a few minutes, and he used his walkie-talkie to report an all-clear message to Rohan, who told us to take the left fork in the trail and meet the company at the next crossroads.

About half an hour later, as our little patrol approached the crossroads, where there were several houses and a large barn, two or three German mortar shells struck near one of the houses. Bailey and his squad went left, toward the shelter of the houses, and my squad and I headed right, toward the large barn, thinking we would find some cover there. Just as we opened a gate to a fenced-in area where several dairy cows were standing around chewing their cuds, two more mortar shells hit the barn roof. We all threw ourselves flat behind a huge pile of manure. It was then that I heard, just behind me, a voice say, "Damn, you fellows sure picked a lousy place to take cover. First time I ever had to hit the dirt in a pile of cow dung."

I looked around, and not twenty yards to our left, peeking over another pile of manure, I saw a helmet with two silver stars on it. I immediately recognized our handsome division commander, Maj. Gen. Willard G. Wyman. I can't remember exactly what we said in reply. After a minute, when it appeared that the shelling had stopped, Wyman stood up, wished us luck, and headed back toward the crossroads, where his jeep and driver were waiting. That was the second and last time I ever found myself close to our general.

With the bloodless capture of Lambach and a large number

A CHANCE MEETING WITH OUR DIVISION COMMANDER

of Germans, I began to feel much more optimistic than I had for the last two months about my chances to see the end of the war without being killed or wounded. The rumor was that tomorrow we would reach our objective—the city of Steyr on the Enns River—and there meet the Russians.

As the crow flies, Steyr is about twenty-five miles almost due east of Lambach. But the distance along the route G Company marched, then rode, was more like thirty-five miles.

Saturday, May 5, started out as a day for high spirits and celebration. We were about to meet the Russians, and from all the evidence we saw that morning, the war in Europe was over. Mussolini was dead, and now we knew from Armed Forces Radio that Adolf Hitler had committed suicide in his bunker in Berlin. All of the Austrian civilians we saw in the towns and on the streets of Steyr that morning were smiling and acting like they had been waiting to be liberated for years—as had the French in Paris the preceding summer. But we knew the difference: The Austrians had been our enemies, while the French had not.

We started out on foot from Lambach that morning with G Company in the lead, marching cross-country through some woods and along a trail until we came to the main highway leading to Steyr. It must have been about 10:00 A.M. when a convoy of empty six-by-six trucks met the company and some other following units of the 2d Battalion as we took a long break. We had no idea that the shooting war was not yet quite over for us.

After we boarded the trucks, our fast-moving convoy followed closely behind jeeps carrying our regimental commander and other officers. As we approached Steyr, the convoy slowed suddenly upon sighting a long, ragtag column of enemy soldiers headed our way on the road. There were a few trucks in that column, towing artillery pieces and heavily loaded trailers, but the majority of the enemy troops were either walking, riding on horseback, or in horse-drawn carts of every description. At first we were struck dumb by the sight, as well as somewhat fearful, because we could see that all those Krauts were still armed.

Up ahead we could hear someone, probably one of the battalion staff officers in a jeep, shouting at the Germans, "Clear the way! Clear the way! *Alles kaput! Krieg* finish!" The lead German trucks willingly pulled over to make room. Then the enemy column stopped as our trucks crawled past at slow speed. Several of my buddies in our truck picked up the chant, "*Alles kaput! Krieg* finish! War over!"

Word was passed back along our line of trucks, "Everybody keep your mouth shut and hold your fire. No shooting unless shot at and an officer gives the order."

OUR CONVOY MEETS A GERMAN COLUMN WEST OF STEYR

Several of the enemy privates armed with rifles grinned, waved, and said, over and over again, "*Ja, ja, Krieg ist zu End. Alles kaput.* War over. *Alles kaput.*" Then several of them made gestures as if they wished to throw their rifles up to us, but we laughed and waved them off. Then we noticed a few sour-faced officers who were wearing pistols. *Those* we wanted as souvenirs! But nothing doing—those arrogant officers all pretended they didn't understand, or they simply ignored us.

Soon we were rolling faster again, down the highway to Steyr. That enemy column must have been almost a mile long, and if so, there were probably at least two thousand German and Austrian soldiers in that group. Had they chosen to open fire, we would have been sitting ducks.

Our convoy finally arrived in the main square of Steyr, a hundred or so yards from the Enns River. We stopped while the regimental officers leading us dismounted and conferred beside the road. Our truck was stopped right next to a radio jeep, and we listened with some awe and admiration as Colonel Wooten himself stood there talking into a radio microphone, probably to the division commander, General Wyman. I distinctly heard him say, "Yes, sir. No resistance. I'm sending the 2d Battalion on across the river."

WE OVERHEAR COL. WOOTEN'S REPORT TO THE GENERAL

As we sat there in our trucks, it seemed that thousands of Austrians, mostly old men, women, and children, waved from the sidewalks and windows. Some threw flowers, just as we had seen the French of Paris do in newsreels. It was surreal.

I was a bit nervous when I heard Wooten say that our 2d Battalion would go on across the river, knowing that we would probably meet the Russians over there. But other than that, I was elated, like all the rest of my buddies, to think that our war was surely over and done with at last. But it was not *quite* over.

It was probably about noon when our convoy crossed the bridge to the east, once again following the regimental jeeps. On a long stretch of highway, with hills rising to our left and right, a battery of dreaded 88s opened fire. I heard a *screech-whoosh-blam* as the first of several shells whizzed by our truck and exploded somewhere to the rear. Then those gunners got the range, and we heard the next two or three shells slam into, or very close to, the jeeps up ahead.

Our trucks instantly braked to a jarring stop, and an officer—it may have been Colonel Wooten himself—ran back along the convoy, pointing and shouting, "Second Battalion off the trucks! Everybody off! George Company, off the road to the left!"

Under Captain Neal's direction, our entire company piled off of our eight or nine trucks as fast as we could and took cover in the culvert on the left side of the road. Bailey's squad and my squad were told to leave our mortars on the truck, and were sent up the ditch to the front of the stalled convoy. We were accompanied by one of the company's machine-gun squads.

A gruesome, never-to-be-forgotten sight sickened me as we ran past the jeep that had been in the lead. It had received a direct hit from an 88, and slumped behind its steering wheel was what was left of the driver—just his bloody, headless torso. On the other side of the road we saw two or three officers, including our battalion executive officer, Maj. Irving Heymont, hunkered down behind a machine gun that was firing short bursts at a line of trees on a hill to the right. As we were to learn later, they were firing at two 88s that were partially hidden up on that hill. Heymont was later awarded the Silver Star for organizing that little ad hoc group of machine gunners.

AMBUSHED!—"SECOND BATTALION OFF THE TRUCKS!"

An officer who had followed us down the ditch ran up to me and pointed to our left—up a barren and slightly muddy slope covered with grass—in the direction of some half-hidden houses and a grove of trees. "Sergeant," he said to me, gasping for breath, "there's two more 88s up in those woods. Take your men up there to those houses and see if you can flank 'em."

I started up that grassy slope and motioned to Decker, Hatley, Vincent, and Packard to spread out and follow. Bailey and his four men ran up to the houses farther over to our left. When we were less than halfway to the first house, another two 88 rounds hit the dirt behind us. I heard Vincent cry, "I'm hit! I'm hit!"

I turned back to look at him. The bipod legs of his BAR had

been blown off, but I could see immediately that he was not hurt badly. He was kneeling, holding his left hand, and looking at it for blood. Meanwhile, Decker, Hatley, and Packard had run on ahead, toward the house. I told Vincent to follow them and we would look at his hand later. He stood up and began to trot on up the slope, with me following. Vincent and I were lucky that those two 88 shells had exploded in the soft, muddy grass on that slope. Because of this, most of the lethal pieces of shrapnel had gone upward in a cone.

As I brought up the rear, I realized that we had not been fired on by the two 88s supposedly hidden in the trees to my right, but by the guns on the hill across the road behind us! As I ran, I thought, *Oh, please God, let me get into that house before they fire again!*

My prayer was answered, but barely. The other men had disappeared into the house through a sheltered entryway to the left. As I ran up to this entrance, I saw a stone wall straight ahead of me. Set back under an arched niche in this wall was a Catholic shrine with a bust of the Virgin Mary. Just as I turned left into the entryway I heard a *screech* and felt a blast behind me. I staggered into the house, my ears ringing. We heard more 88 rounds hit outside; then the firing stopped.

After a few minutes I decided it was safe to venture outside. I saw that the shrine had been destroyed by a direct hit.

That old house where I had my last close encounter with death was on the outskirts of Niederglink (Lower Glink), just across the Enns River from Steyr.

The rest of G Company soon came up the slope and joined us there. Before we proceeded into the village proper, we passed another scene of carnage, in a ravine just below where the two other 88s were sitting, abandoned. In that ravine were the bodies of several German or Austrian artillerymen, and it was clear from the evidence how they had died. The other two 88s that

LAST CLOSE SHAVE—AN 88 SHELL SMASHES A SHRINE

had fired at us from their position maybe half a mile on the other side of the road had inadvertently knocked out their own buddies manning the two guns in the Niederglink woods!

As our column advanced into that little village, we experienced the final deadly act in our war. It was the last time I fired my M1 rifle in combat. Shortly after we started up the main street, we heard the sound of a light plane engine from somewhere in the direction we were headed, and then I saw it—a Fiesler Storch light plane—climbing low over the rooftops of the houses at the street's end. As the plane banked our way, we instinctively snapped the safeties off of our weapons and waited.

I was peering around the corner of a house, in the shadow of its wall, when I caught a brief glimpse of it coming, and I managed to get off one quick shot at it before it banked overhead to my rear. Then I heard the clatter of a submachine gun. I looked out into the center of the main street, and there stood our tall, broad-beamed company commander, Capt. Herbert V. Neal, firing his tommy gun straight up into the air.

The next thing I knew, there was an explosion near where Neal stood, and when I looked, a huge ball of flame and smoke rose from a large tree. When the smoke cleared, I could see the remains of the Storch; one wheel dangled below a branch, and the rest of the plane was crumpled and burning in the treetop. A few GIs ran up to that tree, but they were driven back by pieces

CAPTAIN NEAL SHOOTS DOWN A GERMAN LIGHT PLANE

of flaming, falling debris. In a few minutes, someone came back from that wreckage and said, "Jesus! Two of 'em, both burned to a crisp. And one of 'em was a woman!"

And for a day or two, the rumor was that the woman in the little plane was none other than Germany's most famous female pilot, Hanna Reich, trying to escape with some Nazi bigwig down to the safety of the Alps. Days later we learned that it could not have been she. She was found alive elsewhere.

My one rifle shot could not have knocked that plane down. Even as I had fired, I knew I had missed. All of the credit goes to Captain Neal, whose full magazine of .45-caliber tommy gun slugs hit the plane's gas tank.

So ended our fifty-seventh day in combat—in truth our last day in any serious danger. But we were officially in combat for the next three days, back in the city of Steyr. One reason was that Russian machine-gun fire came across the Enns River now and then, and we also fired our own machine guns to prevent the enemy from crossing to our side at night. Another was that on May 8, a trigger-happy member of G Company fired one last shot at the German enemy.

May 6 was a Sunday; all the church bells of Steyr rang morning, noon, and night. It didn't occur to me to look for a Protestant church to attend, and anyway, I was too busy organizing a guard detail for our street and the nearby bridge.

The next day, May 7, was spent arranging for the care and disposition of thousands of displaced persons of all nationalities who were found in several nearby concentration camps. That night I was with a guard detail in a bunker on the river's edge. Now and then we spotted a few Russians on the other side of the river, riding motorcycles with sidecars, entering house after house. From time to time we heard their submachine guns chatter. Later we learned that these troops were mostly illiterate peasants who were allowed a few days to loot, burn, and rape, before they were withdrawn and replaced by better and more disciplined Russian army units.

On Tuesday, May 8, 1945, the war in Europe officially ended. As part of an American-Russian agreement, from that day on no enemy troops or civilians were allowed to cross the river to our side, to escape the Russians. To ensure this, we set up machine guns along the west bank of the Enns and at the bridges, and at set intervals, or whenever something suspicious was seen in the river, we fired machine-gun bursts into the water. The Russians did the same.

That afternoon, when I was temporarily sergeant of the guard at one of the bridges, I saw an open German staff car approach with white flags flying. The GI who stood in the roadway was a kid named Keefer, who had been temporarily assigned to my guard detail. He raised his bayoneted rifle and hollered, *"Halt! Halt!"* When the stupid driver didn't stop, Keefer shot out the vehicle's front tire!

Colonel Wooten and a few other regimental officers arrived shortly, and I heard Wooten give the German general in that car—Lt. Gen. Lothar von Rendulic, commander of the German Army Group South—the following order: "We will not accept your surrender until you go back, locate, and return to us our Captain Rafferty, who we understand was captured by your troops yesterday."

Captain Rafferty was our battalion's S-2, or intelligence officer. On May 7 he had led a patrol of the 71st Reconnaissance Troop across the river to make contact with the Russians. The upshot of this episode was that, after the German staff car's flat tire was changed, the Kraut bigwigs went back across the bridge, and that night our Captain Rafferty came back, with von Rendulic and the other Kraut officers with him. General Wyman was there to meet them, and the surrender of all the troops under von Rendulic's command was arranged.

Early the next foggy morning, May 9, we saw a ghostly Russian in a long overcoat, with a rifle and a long bayonet attached, standing guard on the other side of a roll of barbed wire our engineers had placed in the center of the bridge. I strolled out to meet him, tried without much success to communicate with him in German, and gave him a cigarette. That was my only contact with our Russian allies.

The house in which my squad was billeted in Steyr during that second week in May 1945 had a bathtub with a gas-fired heater above the faucets. Hot water at last! I took at least one bath each day that week. After sixty days with nothing more than an infrequent sponge bath, at last I was clean! We were also blessed with our own servant—a cheerful Austrian *Hausfrau*. My field jacket required three washings by that old washerwoman before all the grime came out. I had walked at least four hundred miles during those sixty days, and the calluses on the bottoms of my feet were so thick I could stick a pin in them and feel nothing.

My feet notwithstanding, oh, how good it felt to be alive after V-E Day in that spring of 1945!

The 71st Infantry Division had the so-called honor of being "the farthest east" of all U.S. combat units in Europe when Germany surrendered unconditionally on May 8, 1945. The war with Japan was to go on for another three months before the dropping of two American atomic bombs ended it.

In Europe, a "point" system was set up to determine which of the several million American GIs there would be sent home for discharge, and who would either stay in Europe as occupation troops, or be sent to the Pacific to help MacArthur win his war there. The points were calculated on the basis of marital status, number of children, length of service, time in the ETO, and time in actual combat.

Several of my married G Company friends were sent home for discharge a month or two after V-E Day. I did not have enough points to be among that lucky group. I was single, not quite twenty-one, with just under two years of service and two months in combat. Several million of us "low-pointer" GIs became part of the U.S. occupation armies. Many of us—especially the combat infantrymen—had another "big drop" to sweat, namely the probability that we would be sent to join the invasion of Japan as soon as transportation was available.

The 71st Infantry Division stayed on occupation duty in the vicinity of Steyr-am-Enns for only a few weeks. In June the division was moved back to the vicinity of Augsburg, in Bavaria, Germany. G Company of the 5th Infantry Regiment spent the next several months of that 1945 summer and fall stationed at a variety of different Bavarian towns with names such as Dinkelscherben, Zusmarshausen, Landsberg, and Wolfratshausen.

Our division had a rest camp on an Alpine foothills lake named the Ammersee, southwest of Munich. Several of us spent a three- or four-day vacation there before returning to the humdrum life of occupation duty. Our chores included manning checkpoints; inspecting refugees' papers as the overloaded trucks on which they rode to whatever destination stopped for the night; and making surprise early-morning raids on German villages and houses to search for weapons, black-market goods, and SS or other Nazi bigwigs.

It was in Dinkelscherben, not long after my twenty-first birthday, that I developed a taste for German beer, and that ended my vow to stay a teetotaler. And it was in early August, during our stay in Zusmarshausen, that the best news we could imagine came to us over Armed Forces Radio: the voice of President Harry S. Truman announced that an atomic bomb had been dropped on Hiroshima!

I shall never forget that morning. Several of us had taken a child's wagon up the hill to a large brewery, bought a barrel of good, cold, German beer, and loaded it on the wagon. Two of us gleefully sat atop that barrel and steered the wagon at a good clip down the road to our house. A dozen or so of us had already guzzled a canteen cup or two of that strong brew as we sat in the sun outside our house and heard Truman's announcement. You can imagine how we tipsy beer drinkers cheered the news!

A few days later, on August 9, we heard that a second atomic bomb had been dropped, on the Japanese city of Nagasaki, and then we learned that Japan had surrendered at last.

Several weeks later, after we had moved to another town,

TIPSY BEER DRINKERS CELEBRATE NEWS OF THE A-BOMB

two G Company GIs borrowed a jeep and made a weekend return trip to Zusmarshausen to visit their girlfriends. One of the
girls invited them to a friend's home, and lo, there on the mantel
above the fireplace, was a photograph of three civilian boys in
white shirts, one with an accordian.

"Hey," said one of the GIs, that guy with the accordian looks
just like Al Feltman!"

Whereupon the elderly owners of the house replied, "Feltman? *Ja, ja,* our name is Feltman, and that boy in the photograph is our nephew Alfred, who went to America in 1938."

What a coincidence! None of us remembered the name of
the Bavarian town where Sergeant Feltman had told us he was
born. And now, just three months after he was killed in the bat-

tle for Germersheim and Lingenfeld, we had unknowingly been stationed right there for a time.

In September 1945 we spent a few weeks stationed in the city of Augsburg, where the 5th Infantry Regiment headquarters was located, then moved again to Landsberg, where Adolf Hitler had once been imprisoned. Then, sometime before Christmas 1945, our company moved to a large Catholic-run spa called Krumbad, just south of the town of Krumbach, about thirty-five miles southwest of Augsburg.

G Company was by this time at half strength, as most of our senior NCOs and older privates had been sent home. My friend Johnny Rohan became first sergeant. I took over the company supply room and was promoted to staff sergeant.

By Christmas 1945 I had almost enough points to be sent home for my discharge. But one night, in the NCO Club in Krumbach, I met and fell in love with the Estonian girl who was to become my first wife. She and her family were "DPs" (displaced persons) who had been living in northern Germany for most of the war, and had, after several harrowing adventures, managed to make their way out of East Germany into the American occupation zone.

The Estonian girl and I became engaged a few weeks after we met, and I signed up to stay in the army for another six months. Our military government rules required a wait of four months before we could marry. Furthermore, the 5th Infantry Regiment was once again sent back down to Austria, and the rules prohibited my fiancée from leaving Germany to accompany me there.

To solve the problem, I arranged to be transferred to the 60th Infantry Regiment, stationed in Ingolstadt, on the Danube River. Before my transfer, our new company commander was thoughtful enough to promote me to the rank of technical sergeant, which meant an increase in pay. We were married in Ingolstadt in May 1946.

The 60th Infantry Regiment had no slots open for platoon sergeants wearing a technical sergeant's stripes, so they gave me the "cushy" job of running the NCO Club in Ingolstadt. I was also assigned the job of regimental entertainment director.

During those relatively pleasant days of being married and managing the NCO Club I got over my negative feelings about my former enemies, the Germans and Austrians. Until then, like many of my buddies, I had tended to demonize all German and Austrian soldiers, not just the SS. It helped immensely that I became friends with a young German ex-infantryman—an amputee named Leo—who was assigned to me as our NCO Club bartender. Leo and I spent many enjoyable hours playing chess and exchanging war stories. This had much to do with my transformation.

Not long after my parents learned of my marriage and my job as NCO Club manager, my mother wrote me a letter saying, "I can just imagine you in the club, standing behind the counter, opening bottles of Coca-Cola and Ginger Ale."

Oh, Mother, I thought. *If you only knew how many barrels of beer and how many bottles of gin, schnapps, and whiskey we open every night!*

In the fall of 1946 my Estonian war bride and I finally arrived in the States. I was discharged at Fort Sheridan, north of Chicago, and we returned to my hometown of Denver, Colorado. That marriage lasted fourteen years. But I was lucky that it brought me a daughter and a grandson.

And thanks to the GI Bill, the U.S. government paid my way through another three years at the University of Colorado. In 1950, armed with an M.S. degree in aeronautical engineering and a private pilot's license—also paid for by the GI Bill—I began a long forty-year career in the U.S. aerospace and defense industry. In 1974 I was happily remarried, and after retiring in 1992 I at last found the time to try my hand at serious writing.

This memoir is my latest product. It would never have been completed without the encouragement and support of my wife, Annie.

ACKNOWLEDGMENTS

For their help and advice over the months it took to finish and polish this book, special thanks go to editors Ron Doering and to Eric Hammel.

Others who have earned my thanks are assistant editors Deirdre Lanning and Tim Mak, book designer Julie Schroeder, and assistant managing editor Crystal Velasquez.

And I am profoundly grateful to E. J. McCarthy and Robert V. Kane for their decision, over two years ago, to publish this work.

© AMY T. JOY

ABOUT THE AUTHOR

Dean P. Joy was born in Denver, Colorado, in 1924. He is retired
and lives in Los Gatos, California. Following his Army service
during World War II, he returned home and used the GI Bill to
complete his college education. In June 1950, after receiving an
MS degree in Aeronautical Engineering from the University of
Colorado, where he specialized in the study of helicopter aerodynamics, he began his forty-two-year career in the aerospace
defense industry. Those years included five at Hiller Helicopters
in Palo Alto, California, as a flight test engineer and later Chief
of Aerodynamics; one year as a helicopter combat operations re-
search consultant to the French Defense Ministry, which included a month on-site in the Algerian combat zone and three
months in Paris; five years managing his own Operations Re-
search Company in Tucson, including a year at Fort Huachuca,
Arizona, where he helped the U.S. Army formulate its original
electronic data processing system; and following this, a final
thirty years with Lockheed Missiles & Space Company in
Sunnyvale, California, as a Systems Analysis Department manager, then Program Manager of a series of Army combat vehicle
design studies, then Senior Systems analyst on a variety of Space
Defense Initiative ("Star Wars") programs.